Praise for *Crossing the Divide*

"Written in a non-academic framework and a breezy, accessible style, Jessica Stone's personal experience brings life and meaning to the cross-cultural skills critical to meaningfully working abroad."

—CLAIRE RAPUANO, RETURNED PEACE CORPS
VOLUNTEER (BENIN 2017–2019)

"As the former Director of the Counterinsurgency Training Center in Afghanistan, I have read a lot of books designed to encourage and teach cross-cultural competency. This one stands out among the crowd. It is easy to read, and full of insights born of both experience—and reflection on that experience—which lead the reader to a better understanding of the internal qualities—and external skills—needed to succeed in an interconnected and globalized workforce."

—COL (RETIRED) JOHN F. AGOGLIA U.S. ARMY,
FORMER DIRECTOR OF COIN TRAINING, KABUL

"Undaunted by the unknown, readers walk with Jessica through a variety of different cultural contexts and learn new skills to become more well-rounded leaders and global citizens. I plan to share *Crossing the Divide* with my mentees and military colleagues."

—COL MYLES B. CAGGINS III, U.S. ARMY,
FORMER SPOKESPERSON AT U.S. CENTCOM

"Cross-cultural mistakes are absolutely inevitable, but there's pleasure here for the reader who will learn just as much from Jessica's mistakes as from her successes."

—JOHN WESTERN, MAXWELL PROFESSOR OF TEACHING EXCELLENCE,
SYRACUSE UNIVERSITY, AUTHOR OF "COSMOPOLITAN EUROPE:
A STRASBOURG SELF-PORTRAIT (HERITAGE, CULTURE
AND IDENTITY)" AND "OUTCAST CAPE TOWN"

"Jessica shares the fruit of experience, challenges and mistakes, and gives us tools to equip us for a cross-cultural future. I can think of no better time than now—a period of national reckoning over domestic divisions—to read ~~this~~ ~~~~~~ ~~~~ home."

—DON R
PRESIDEN

D1416956

TIVE &
ITUTE

"Jessica Stone has stood at the crossroads of East and West. In an era where political pundits boil down the U.S.-China competition into Cold War cliches, Jessica brings much-needed nuance and perspective in explaining the most consequential bilateral relationship in the 21st century. With each chapter, she provides the reader with cross-cultural lessons to navigate an increasingly complex world."

—LELAND LAZARUS, SPEECHWRITER AT U.S. SOUTHCOM &
FORMER U.S. DIPLOMAT IN CHINA & THE CARIBBEAN

"I am especially glad this book encourages the next generation of cross-cultural practitioners. We don't need a crystal ball to know the future of business, diplomacy, and scientific exploration will hinge on our ability to express and communicate values effectively. With her book in hand, hard-earned lessons on humility and grace will undoubtedly smooth the road for those embarking on their own adventures—be they far from home or just down the street."

—KRISTEN FARNUM, CONFLICT RESOLUTION TRAINER,
FOREIGN SERVICE INSTITUTE, DEPT. OF STATE

"Having bridged cultural and religious divides across the planet for a number of years, I've learned that the most effective way to do so is by developing a sense of empathy with the other party. In short, doing the hard work of understanding why they view the problem the way they do and proceeding from there. In many respects, this is exactly what Jessica is suggesting as the key ingredient in her own work dealing with these same kinds of boundaries. It is an honor to welcome her into the ranks of those authors who are dealing with this subject matter in a penetrating and insightful way. Beyond the lessons learned, *Crossing the Divide* is a pleasure to read and I recommend it highly for anyone interested in promoting reconciliation in a troubled world."

—DR. DOUGLAS M. JOHNSTON, JR., PRESIDENT EMERITUS & FOUNDER
OF THE INTERNATIONAL CENTER FOR RELGION & DIPLOMACY

CROSSING
THE DIVIDE

Patty—
Keep the
faith!
♡ Jessica
Anne

CROSSING
THE DIVIDE

20 LESSONS TO HELP YOU THRIVE IN
CROSS-CULTURAL ENVIRONMENTS
2nd Edition

JESSICA STONE

Stone Productions, LLC

Crossing the Divide: 20 Lessons to Help You Thrive in Cross-Cultural Environments
© 2021 by Stone Productions, LLC. 2nd edition, December 2021.

ISBN 978-1-7364508-3-3

Cover art design by Bedro Brand Box, LLC
Interior design by lindseybeharry.com
Interior photography credits: Jessica Stone, Richard and Wendy Weinstein, Abbas Daiyar, Véronique Soutenet

Printed in the United States of America

To my husband Daniel,
Thank you for listening to these stories for years
and for supporting my effort to commit them, along with the
lessons they hold, to paper.

To my parents,
Thank you for nurturing in me the curiosity to understand
and for instilling in me the tools to discover.

To my daughters, Charlotte and Jourdan,
It's my hope that future generations—including yours—will be
inspired to understand and engage with those different from themselves
in the pursuit of a more clear understanding of truth. Remember my
loves—every person has intrinsic value and every person's perspective
is important to understand. We can accomplish greater things
together than apart.

CONTENTS

ACKNOWLEDGMENTS

I WOULD LIKE TO THANK those who taught me and challenged me to be more culturally aware and forgave me when I fell short. Among them: Richard and Wendy Weinstein, my brother Josh, Binnie Weinstein, Siv Cacamis, Jorgen, Gunilla, Sofia and Anna Kagelind, Gary Miles, Deb Kline-Smith, Verena Vogt, Véronique Soutenet, Tamara Theissen, Benoît Fink, Elizabeth Goodman, and Christine Kozikowski.

To my forever friends in Afghanistan: Ahmad Shuja, Abbas Daiyar, Reza Kateb, and Abbas Changezi my deepest gratitude to you for sharing your world and perspectives with me. A special thanks as well to Colonel (Ret.) John Agoglia. Your perspective and involvement in this book project have been invaluable.

To Rod and Mary Macalister, your continued friendship, mentorship, and cross-cultural adventure planning continue to inspire. You live life the way it should be lived!

To World Relief, Compassion International, and World Vision—thank you for including me in your efforts to make a difference!

To Niu Yun, Ching-Yi Chang, Wang Guan, Li Xiang, Cheng Lei, and so many other Chinese colleagues who have taught me a boatload, I'm grateful.

To my faithful partners in prayer, Jennifer Scholle, Vanessa Peters, Maria Buck, Heather Hill Dunn, Kelley Harris Meshirer, my heartfelt thanks.

I'd also like to thank Katie Ruel Riess and Meredith Eaton for giving me the tools to put these lessons to paper in a format that can benefit others. Your Publishing & Publicity Mastermind was a crucial step toward launching this project. I could not have done this without you.

To my editor, Leilani Squires, you made the message sharper and brighter. To Lindsey Beharry, I'm blessed by your talent, and to Kelly Bedrossian, thank you for turning ideas into action.

FOREWORD

Rodney J. MacAlister

international executive
serial self-reinventor

FOR NEARLY 30 YEARS, the Tchimpounga Chimpanzee Reha-
bilitation Centre has provided a safe, wild habitat for nearly 200 or-
phaned chimpanzees in the Republic of the Congo. Many were initially
rescued from starvation at the Brazzaville Zoo and later liberated from
the illegal bushmeat and pet animal trades. But Tchimpounga would
never have come to fruition if two people from seemingly polar opposite vantage points had not sought and discovered common ground: a
shared love of nature. Those two people are the esteemed conservation-
ist and activist, Dr. Jane Goodall, and myself, Rod MacAlister, international executive and serial self-reinventor.

You see, I built that sanctuary for Dr. Goodall.

At the time, I was fresh into my first experience of running an oil
company in Africa. Nobody around me caught the vision for that stand-
out environmental contribution—not the government, the public, or
my own employees. They could not understand why we should spend
nearly one million dollars on a bunch of chimpanzees when schools had
no desks or blackboards. Fair question.

But as I told the producers of the beautifully depicted Earth Day 2020 film, *The Hope*, by National Geographic, Jane "goes for the kind of change the world is hungry for." And so, with the help of my dedicated colleagues led by Steve Matthews, we turned her vision into a reality. Tchimpounga now represents the largest such fully safe area in Africa where animals can live in the wild. Conservationists come from around the world to study how it was done. Jane and I remain friends to this day.

If you've picked up this book, you may be on your own cross-cultural adventure—or contemplating one. Maybe you've experienced your own cultural barriers, mistakes, limited understanding, or skewed perceptions that have caused you to seek skills to bridge the divides you encounter in your own life. Maybe you're wondering how to move forward in the world in a way that invites unity, mutual understanding, and peace.

My own path is littered with mistakes—in fact many, since I've been crossing divides a long time. But possessing and improving cross-cultural skills—the very tools outlined within these pages—can often mean the difference between success and failure. Sometimes even survival.

Diplomats' practice of cross-cultural skills throughout history has preserved countless lives. It's how the US avoided nuclear conflict with the USSR during the Cold War. During those 45 years, the US and USSR made careful, well-informed judgments about each other. Fear of miscalculation was motivated by the certainty of mutually assured destruction. So, we worked to maintain mutual understanding and communication, despite our profound disagreements.

I often wonder if today's generation of leaders has the same dedication to understand the psychology, motivations and—shall I say—the music to which others dance. I believe Jessica Stone offers a critical toolkit to those leaders.

When I met Jessica 15 years ago, I was impressed with her keen interest in pushing her own boundaries, risking interpersonal challenge, and bridging cultural divides. It's safe to predict this book will make hers a voice—in the sometimes too-faint calls in our world—for more concerted mutual exploration, acceptance, and understanding.

As we look to a future where more global and cultural conflict is anticipated, I am grateful to Jessica for writing *Crossing the Divide*. A world without these skills is moving toward a reality that raises the stakes of needless interpersonal friction with the potential to create violent miscalculation—especially between the US and China, and among the American body politic itself.

On this vital skill, I treasure my privilege of having served at the International Center for Religion and Diplomacy (ICRD) under its founder, my friend and colleague, Doug Johnston. ICRD is dedicated to the imperative that boundaries must be bridged, particularly the divisions created by different religions. As a vital approach to peacemaking across the boundary of religion, ICRD has borne much fruit—an art previously neglected by professional diplomats who now embrace it.

I write this foreword out of great concern for a defining paradox of our time: just as technology is shrinking the world, insularity and polarization are growing. The world cannot descend into millions of stovepipes; only calamity awaits as the logical extension. It is incumbent on each living person to be able to converse with the other; to see his/her point of view; to see what history, culture, experiences inform that view; and to find common ground. Jessica touches on a skill that is not a nice-to-have but is vital for human progress and the advancement of global civilization.

While *Crossing the Divide* is well-reflective of the academic research, Jessica understands the seriousness of the matter and makes it accessible by inviting you into a conversation drawn from her personal experiences. This remarkable lady—a journalist dedicated to reporting the truth objectively—employs her profound gifts of equally high intellectual and emotional intelligence to take us on a cross-cultural exploration around the globe through 20 stories all told with wit and self-effacing charm.

As you get ready to take the next step on your own journey, I want you to hear something unmistakably: cross-cultural competency is for everyone. And Jessica will lead the way in teaching you this skill. While you may draw different lessons from Jessica's own, as you read through these pages you'll be captivated, encouraged, challenged, instructed, and ultimately set loose to seize your own lessons. That's what Jessica does. And that's what *Crossing the Divide* is all about.

INTRODUCTION

THIS BOOK WAS BORN from a lifetime of experiences (so far), adventures, and mishaps which taught me lessons about cross-cultural understanding and competency. Some I learned the easy way. Most I learned by making mistakes and figuring out a better approach in hindsight. I'm not coming from a place of expertise, or having mastered it all, but from a series of experiences I believe can be informative and helpful.

For the purposes of this book, I define "cross-cultural" as literally across ethnic, religious, gender, regional, and organizational boundaries.

These lessons present helpful observations about navigating various environments as you work toward a common goal with others who are different from you, especially in our increasingly interconnected world. I want to help you to "play well in the sandbox." In some cases, these lessons will help you get into the sandbox, especially if it's hundreds of miles away and very different culturally from your American context.

Enjoy the adventure! And please write me back with your own observations at info@jessica-stone.com

Chapter 1

A DAMN YANKEE IN DIXIE

Mobile, Alabama

1980–1985

I AM THE CHILD of a Jewish hippie and a Catholic hippie, both from Long Island, New York. They got married in San Francisco in the 1970s at the height of the sexual revolution. They had moved to the West Coast in part to escape the influences of their families.

They both came to faith through the Jesus Movement and converted to Protestant, Evangelical Christianity. This was not a tame or low-key conversion—it was radical. So much so that my father's mother, Binnie Weinstein, flew out to California to try and stop them from getting married. (She never owned up to it, but that's the story I got when I grew older.)

Cultural differences defined my life from the day I drew my first breath. Ever since I can remember, I've been living in the third person performing the duties of both lead actor and director as I navigated diverse waters. Being born into a family where Jewish and Catholic heritage mixed with a new Protestant faith created one layer of divergent customs. But my parents' decision to move from progressive San

PICTURED: (Top-L) Me at 2 years old. (Top-R) Curiosity begins at home. (Bottom) Me and Mom. Note the everpresent bow in my hair.

Francisco to traditional Mobile, Alabama, added an additional layer of complexity. And I didn't quite fit in to say the least.

I mean, look at me. I'm wearing a t-shirt my Bubbe (grandma) gave me announcing I'm The Bagel Kid (*page 20*). What other child in the 1980s South even knew what a bagel was? I never saw another Alabama kid wear a similar shirt. But here I am!

My dad attended medical school in Mobile and finished residency at a local hospital. My mom was an incredibly creative and vibrant homemaker and home-educator. She even convinced the Mobile *Press-Register* to give her the end of the newspaper rolls from the printing presses for free so we could have an art studio in our little carport. Just add water to the tempera paint powder, mix with cheap paint brushes, and we were on our way to achieving Picasso status!

Between a free-spirit, artistic mother and a bookworm, pocket-protector-wearing physician father, I was brought up to use my brain, ask questions, think deeply, and take risks to create something new.

I was raised in a super strict, conservative, Southern Christian church. Men and women had defined roles. But there were plenty of cultural expectations I never fully lived up to. Despite being born a "Southern belle," in Dixieland, I possessed a Yankee spirit. That meant playing with the boys over playing with dolls, being naturally loud in a culture where children are seen and not heard, and feeling drawn to an international worldview amid a rigid, narrow, and highly domestic early education.

I got used to being different than my peers. And when you're different long enough, you embrace it. It becomes part of your identity. Over time, I grew to see it as a blessing instead of a curse.

All my memories of my first seven years growing up in Mobile, Alabama, are shrouded by an overwhelming sense of being "other." It seemed every instinct I had was the wrong behavior expected of a little girl.

Bows, smocked dresses? Not for me. I'd rather get dirty, throw rocks, be rowdy, unruly, and loud.

Girls should be pretty, dainty, and coiffed? Nope! I'd rather be smart, tough, and gritty. In fact, I'd rather moon the neighbors. (Rest assured, there was a spanking waiting for me after that one!)

My dreams of being a stage actress on New York City's Broadway weren't exactly encouraged by those outside my family.

My Jewish father developed a strong Christian faith, but he was still grappling with his ethnic identity and wanted his children to experience it. So, at Passover and Hanukkah, we traded our fried shrimp and hush puppies for a family dinner of *matzoh*, wine, *challah* bread, the occasional brisket, and some potato *latkes* (whatever the holiday required) to join with Jews around the world in celebrating these traditions.

Except I didn't know anyone else who did what we did. I thought it was weird. I didn't want to be the kid eating these strange foods and saying these foreign prayers. But there I was, doing it anyway.

Somehow, I learned to accept my discomfort with the discordant notes of cultures clashing both within my family and in my interactions with my peers. If I was destined to be different from my friends, it was up to me to accept it and fold it into my sense of self.

But it didn't come without feeling alone and left out. Many everyday experiences which seemed easy and natural for the Southern-born Bible-belters around me felt contrived and forced to me.

Years later, I recall returning to Mobile to visit the church and church school: a place where few certified teachers taught, where the classes posed no challenge to my young brain, and where the behavioral norms felt oppressive. The weight of remembering how ostracized I felt in that culture of oversimplification, willful ignorance, and Southern pride nearly took my breath away.

Even 10 years later, the heaviness of what that place and early chapter of my life represented felt like a crushing burden. I sobbed, feeling a deep emotion I've only since experienced through loss or a broken heart.

I wish I could say I carried that level of understanding and compassion into other interactions I had with people from other cultures, religions, and backgrounds. I didn't. But I do think my early exposures to these differences became a strength that shaped my life, learning, and experience in critical ways.

▶ LESSON 1

You won't understand other cultures if you
don't understand your own. Learning about
what made my culture and lifestyle different
from those around me when I was young
prepared me to adapt to other cultures.

Chapter 2

SMALL TOWN OPPORTUNITY

Lititz, Pennsylvania

1993 – 1996

"" **MY LIFE IS OVER!** I'm going to be stuck delivering pizza for the rest of my life in this backwater town!" I wept in an emotional outburst any parent of a 14-year-old girl has probably experienced first-hand.

There were no 24-hour grocery or drugstores where we had just moved. Lititz, Pennsylvania, possessed no shopping malls within biking distance of our neighborhood—not even a movie theater close to our town. Instead, there were old brick facades and rolling hills dotted with cows and horses. It was just like the idyllic and nostalgic Amish Country brochure pictures which try to entice visitors for a weekend getaway or a family reunion. To a teenager, it was boring, uninteresting and more akin to a prison sentence than a golden opportunity.

Add to that the constant smell of animal excrement, which hung heaviest in the air during humid summer days. Yuck! I would later be able to identify whether it was cows, horses, or chickens producing those foul odors.

We had just left the relative sophistication of Oakland County, Michigan, the seventh wealthiest county in the country, where we lived for seven years after Mobile. In that culture, I attended school with the well-off, entitled kids of car executives. On their 16th birthdays, many received a fully loaded American-made Ford or GMC, tricked out with all the modern bells and whistles one could ever want.

I rubbed shoulders with child models, actresses and actors with film credits, and tennis players primed to go professional. It was the heady materialism of the 1980s, and this community had cash to burn. No one seemed to lack anything in the way of posessions, though maybe in the way of authentic relationships. Drugs were easy to come by, designer clothes were seemingly on every teenager, and it felt like fame was attainable (even without a social media following).

Plucking me out of that environment and planting me in the rolling farm fields of Lancaster County, Pennsylvania, was a complete culture shock. What I didn't appreciate then was the slower pace and more rural set of opportunities you can't get in more developed and urban areas. In Pennsylvania, I met kids with the middle-class values of hard work, authenticity, and self-reliance that were missing among those I went to school with in Michigan.

The class differences played out in other ways, too. The 1990s materialist obsession wasn't within reach for these students. They couldn't argue and tease about the latest brands of jeans and sneakers. Every high school has its cool and uncool kids, its haves and have-nots. But I don't remember gaps between those differences being as huge as they were among the child models, car executive kids, and environment of instant-gratification in the wealthy Detroit suburbs.

In many ways, these students in Lititz, Pennsylvania, had a simpler and more kind experience even while not immune to the dangers of drugs, alcoholism, and teenage pregnancy.

But I was drawn to the one fish swimming upstream—Mr. Gary Miles, my English and composition teacher. He was considered a provocateur because of his support for unions, progressive politics, and separation of church and state.

While the debates in his class weren't exactly rowdy or radical by today's standards, it was in Mr. Miles's class where we learned our opinions could be our own and that all of them deserve to be defended. It was also a safe place to try on different ideas and debate them without fear of retribution. Since these ideals were important to me, too, I found it even more refreshing to find a place where I could sharpen my arguments.

I got my confidence on Mrs. Kline-Smith's stage. She was, and is, a larger-than-life woman with huge dreams and ideas for stage productions. These pushed the meager talents of a bunch of high school students to the edge, but gave us all a sense of accomplishment when we pulled off what started off as a mission impossible.

From the ashes of my teenage despair, I came to experience the best three years of my adolescence—traveling all around the world, singing and dancing, trying new things, forming friendships that have lasted decades, and discovering a sense of self and who I wanted to be. All this directed me toward a future profession.

All that happened as I released my expectations of what my new environment should be and accepted the actual reality.

It also launched me into an early love of travel. At age 16, I sang and danced from the rural high school stage of Mrs. Kline-Smith all the way to France, Germany, Austria, Belgium, Switzerland, and Italy.

From singing sacred music in the halls of the great Duomo Cathedral during Catholic mass in Florence; to regaling a small German town in Bavaria with swing music and classic American patriotic tunes; to having the opportunity at age 16 to actually tour and experience the infamous Dachau Concentration Camp, it turns out moving to a small town was my door to a much wider world.

PICTURED:
My highschool
performing days.

▶ LESSON 2

Don't act on your first read of a new cultural situation. Preconceived notions can blind you to its benefits and beauty. Every environment has something to offer. In my case, I discovered small towns can provide more opportunity with less pressure.

Chapter 3

THE HAWKS AND THE DOVES

Washington, D.C.

Summer, 1996

WHEN I WAS A SENIOR in high school, I received a piece of mail that changed the course of my life. A non-profit in Washington, D.C. was holding a training on how to break into television news. Somehow, in the early age of targeted mail, I showed up on a list to be recruited.

The glossy brochure boasted shiny television screens, testimonials of successful television journalists, and seminars full of bright-eyed student journalists all destined to be the next Katie Couric or Barbara Walters. The classes were developed and taught by a prominent Pittsburgh television anchor who came to Washington, D.C. several times a year to impart his wisdom about getting a job in the mysterious world of television.

I eagerly signed up and spent a weekend in various Washington, D.C. hotel seminar rooms absorbing everything I could about creating my resume, forming a resume tape (yes, they were tapes in those days), leaving a strong first impression during internship interviews, and finding ways to learn the craft for free. I took copious notes and left buoyed by the belief that I was now armed with the tools needed to break into the biz.

I must have stood out in some way because by the end of my senior year, I was offered a paid internship by the education institution which had sponsored the seminar. I could live in paid housing, take classes on politics and political theory, and help support the same seminars I had so eagerly attended.

I was humbled and overwhelmed with gratitude watching my dreams come true. As a person of faith I prayed about all my decisions. I had felt an early leaning, some might label it a "calling," to journalism. Like Mr. Miles, my high school composition teacher, I embraced being counterculture. In my case, this meant being a person of faith launching head-long into secular media which didn't often reflect the values I held dear.

For context, over the summer of that year, MSNBC would launch on July 15, 1996 and *Fox News Channel* launched on October 7, 1996. But that spring news viewers were still largely limited to the three main broadcast channels: NBC, ABC, and CBS. CNN, which led the way in cable news, started operations in 1980. There was no channel marketed to the heartland—to those who were hard-working, traditional, and whose politics are shaped by their religious beliefs.

When the Pittsburgh anchor said his purpose was to help objective and fair journalists successfully land employment, I believed I would be one of them. I thought the best way to pursue that goal was heading to Washington, D.C. and learning all I could about politics, political journalism, and the ways of our nation's capital—to master the art of covering it with fairness and objectivity.

It was one of the largest internship classes they ever had. So many young men and women were selected that there wasn't enough space for us all to live at the intern house. I was fortunate to be among the five women assigned to the solution: to share a two-bedroom furnished apartment in Clarendon, Virginia. It was my first time in high-rise living, and it was exhilarating. The building had a pool on the top floor and a dry cleaners in the bottom. At 17 years old, I thought I had arrived.

And I had, but it was not nirvana. I was about to run head-long into a culture clash of a different sort. My fellow interns were not there to be objective, fair journalists. I was in the one part of the institute which had that objective. The rest of the interns were there to learn how to persuade, fundraise, grassroots organize, and in general use their black and white view of the world to win hearts, minds, and votes to their political point of view. President Ronald Reagan's legacy was omnipresent. He was revered as a leader who stood up to communism, guarded personal liberties, and fought for religious rights and those of the unborn.

I was in the mix with future elected leaders from all over the world, but particularly from the most southern and conservative parts of the United States. They debated (often loudly) the differences between conservative political thought and libertarian political thought in great detail. Some went on to be legislators in their home states; others in their home nations.

Among the American interns, there was little to no appreciation for the cultures of Europe and its influence on us when we were a fledgling nation. Only that they were further down the path to socialism and must thus be learned from in that context. This rubbed hard against my love for all things French and my deep attachment to my European roots.

I naturally gravitated toward the three non-native English speakers, an Austrian, a Czech, and a Chilean. I also met one of my life-long friends, Kelley Harris Meshirer, there. I found solace in conversations with someone for whom the world was not such a black and white world of good guys and bad guys, of communist liberals and patriotic conservatives. We had a more nuanced view of the world born of our journalism backgrounds, and the keen understanding that any political ideology can be co-opted and used for evil. We held common ground in faith and traditional values and felt strongly that there was a need for people with those qualities to serve in secular environments, including the media and government.

I chafed at the absolutism of the course work, which included *Conscience of a Conservative* by Barry Goldwater and Milton Friedman's *Capitalism and Freedom*. While I didn't find the ideas totally anathema, the reverence with which these authors and conservative thinkers were treated had an air of deification. I had never revered anyone that much aside from God. It felt heretical.

Then came the day where part of my assignment was to write a piece of political direct mail. The objective was to cram as much hyperbole and fear into an eight by ten-inch piece of paper so the person reading it had no choice but to write a check. It was the furthest thing from journalism I could think of at the time.

I still don't know how I squeaked by that assignment. Suffice it to say, no checks were written on my behalf because my letter was much too objective and fair to make anyone want to do anything—except perhaps tell my internship coordinator to have me write a news article instead. It solidified my desire to avoid opinion journalism at all costs and to be a journalist who could be trusted to impart the truth to the best of my ability.

This had a profound impact on me personally and professionally. I held to the words of the Pittsburgh anchor that objectivity and fairness were the currency of good journalism. It would be those qualities, and a lot of chutzpah and perseverance, which would help me succeed in this highly competitive field. It was an ethos I carried with me to Syracuse University and its top-notch journalism school.

The Hawks and the Doves

I named this chapter the Hawks and the Doves because I saw the animated politicos around me as the hawks who wanted to kill the bad ideas, while I wanted to simply understand ideas contrary to my own in order to fairly portray them in my writing. The Hawk and Dove is also a well-known bar on Capitol Hill that has been around since the Carter administration. It's been the backdrop for many a compromise of politicians when compromise was a value that was sought in our nation's congress. For my part, beers and conversations there helped me bridge the gap between the ideologues and ultimately better portray them and their perspectives in subsequent journalistic efforts.

▶ LESSON 3

When you encounter a culture clash, seek the lesson. Once you've identified it, decide whether remaining in that culture requires you to betray a fundamental personal value. If so, it's better to appreciate what you've learned and move on rather than remaining in constant internal conflict.

Chapter 4

MEETING JESSICA WEINSTEIN

Syracuse, New York

2000–2006

GREW UP WITH a North Star sense of my own personal faith as a Christian, but a very multi-layered sense of who I was ethnically and culturally. While studying at Syracuse University, my last name was Weinstein. It was, as I often joked, analogous to having the last name of "Smith" in more Anglo-Saxon circles. The combination of my first and last name was so common that I once received the bank account statement of another Jessica Weinstein by mistake. There were three of us on campus my freshman year.

During college, I babysat for a family engaged in the traditions of Messianic Judaism, a sort of bridge between Jewish cultural traditions and Christian doctrine. It was part of my early exposure to other families who, like mine, mixed Christian and Jewish customs. It gave me an alternative point of view as to how others combine these strands into a cord. It ultimately wasn't a fit for me, but it became an important part of my journey to understand how these faith traditions and religions shaped me.

PICTURED:
Grandma Binnie
Weinstein and I
through the years.

I graduated and took a job as a local television reporter in Utica, New York. I also began to pursue a deeper relationship with my paternal grandmother, Binnie Weinstein. She lived alone on Long Island, had a big group of friends, was involved in extensive volunteer commitments, and had a distinct identity in the secular Jewish community of Hicksville, New York. She had lived a wild and courageous life, spanning from sharecropping in the Catskill mountains, to faking residency to get a college degree in Manhattan, to being deployed to Guam as a United States Navy nurse during World War II, to meeting my grandfather at a progressive party (read communist) meeting after the war.

It didn't end there. She and my grandfather continued their travels and adventures after their kids were grown. She always embodied the natural curiosity and chutzpah which I desired to emulate.

Grandma and I rarely discussed our actual thoughts on religious conviction. Ironically, her lack of faith and my strong, resolute faith didn't always conflict. She taught me through her actions that I could take my faith with me no matter where I went.

She was my door to New York's Jewish culture. I was welcomed to join it with her even though I was a professing Christian.

When my father initially became a Christian before I was born, my grandmother made the radical decision to push against what her culture imposed on her. Instead of cutting him out of her life due to a sense of betrayal to the traditions she'd raised him in, she decided no matter what my father believed, he would always be her son. In that moment, she also left room for the possibility of one day knowing her grandchildren.

Years later, my grandmother and I went together to museums and ballets, Broadway shows, and bar and bat mitzvahs. We celebrated Passover Seders for many years with her secular, progressive, Jewish friends and neighbors. I grew into young adulthood more comfortable in my multiethnic skin. I became familiar with this rich tapestry of older Jewish intellectuals and their views on everything from film to fashion.

Cultivating a deep and meaningful relationship with Grandma Binnie gave me the opportunity to discover what we had in common and how we could learn from each other.

I'll never forget the many times we flipped through old black and white photographs of her time serving in Guam as a Navy nurse. One of those pictures was of a broadly smiling young woman dressed in her uniform, her curly hair peeking out from beneath her cap. I saw my own face staring back at me. She never stopped telling anyone who would listen that I thought I looked like her. But "Jessica is much prettier," she would add.

These experiences seeped into my own sense of personhood in a way which rounded out my story. I finally knew and understood more of my heritage and identity. I could determine for myself how I would bridge these inherent internal contradictions. It was important to me to explore the cultural differences around me and to celebrate them. My name telegraphed a persona that was Jewish, Yankee, and urban. Someone initially meeting me naturally had one set of expectations and assumptions of who I was, only to discover those were not at all on the mark.

In Utica, I adamantly said "Happy Holidays" as opposed to "Merry Christmas." I took it upon myself to do a series of holiday reports featuring the cultural and religious diversity of the Utica area, showing how families celebrated Jewish Hanukkah, Roman Catholic and Italian Christmas, and the Polish traditions of the Feast of St. Nicolaus. When my general manager (the most senior manager at a televisions station) offered me tickets to the High Holy Days services at his temple, I accepted. I then faked my way through the Hebrew call and response. Ironically, I earned a compliment on my "excellent Hebrew." I finally clarified my religious dating preferences before the general manager set me up on a blind date with a nice Jewish boy from that temple.

I was embarking on a season of discovery set in motion by my increased proximity to so many Jewish people and cultural landmarks.

I'd never had this kind of open access to Jewish culture, food, and faith traditions. In Syracuse, Utica, and Rochester, New York, it was much easier to find. So easy I didn't have to look—it found me. For example, when I took a reporter job in Rochester, New York, I lived on the same street as the Jewish Federation. My first week on the air, I got a telephone call from the Federation asking if I wanted to attend services for Rosh Hashanah and Yom Kippur. There were times I fielded calls from viewers assuming my religion and expressing a desire to set me up with a nice young man they knew (his profession was always mentioned, especially when it was a doctor or lawyer).

In another twist, I discovered a whole new part of my extended Jewish family who lived in Rochester, bringing me even closer to those traditions and cultural assumptions. They had intermarried with other faiths and did not take their religion as seriously as they did their culture and ethnic identities. But here, too, was another way of combining the faith traditions I had been raised around.

The most difficult aspect of bridging this divide was finding I didn't completely belong in either place, despite the most loving and well-meaning sense of community extended to me by the Jewish and Christian camps. Yet, while I couldn't always be my authentic self in these settings, I could authentically be a student of those around me.

That became my path forward and fundamentally set me up to be a better cross-cultural communicator and affirmed my profession as a journalist.

▶ LESSON 4

When you approach others with what you have in common or what you know and celebrate about their culture or identity, they are far more open to relationship and an exchange of ideas. Finding commonality is the key and is becoming a lost art. Don't let it fade away.

Chapter 5

COLD SHOULDER IN STRASBOURG

Strasbourg, France

1998–1999

AS I PREPARED TO board the Air France flight to Paris, and eventually to Strasbourg, I knew what I had to do: immerse myself in this new culture and language to achieve my goal of thinking, speaking, and even dreaming in my second language. Even after 10 years of study, I still didn't feel I had crossed the final threshold to French fluency.

From the moment I set foot on the aircraft, I was determined to speak only French with the flight attendants and anyone else I came across. The impact of that choice is not unlike jumping into the deep end of a swimming pool and choosing to swim with only one arm or one leg. It's a self-inflicted hardship, especially amongst native French speakers with an awareness, but no mastery, of your mother tongue.

Along with the hardship came a sort of loneliness, forcing me to be more of an observer of, than an actor in the events around me.

Initially, I could no longer have casual conversations or even go to coffee with someone I knew wouldn't want to speak French with me. I had to rehearse what I would say in advance before ordering coffee.

PICTURED: Me and my dear friend, Véronique Soutenet, in Dijon, France, 1999.

Lucky for me, the French rarely, if ever, break into English. It was before the Euro became the common currency, and the European Union was young.

Even so, when someone did speak to me in English, I would do my best to insist on keeping the conversation in French. It was exhausting at first. I would fall into an early evening silence, incredibly uncharacteristic of me, out of sheer fatigue. But there were also positives to this approach.

Before taking the entrance exam to the Institut International d'Etudes Françaises (IIEF) at the Université de Strasbourg, I spent a four-day weekend with my pen pal and best French friend, Véronique Soutenet, in Dijon where she went to university. We had met years earlier when she stayed with my family for two weeks during a high school exchange. We became fast friends and have remained in touch ever since. When we visit each other periodically, we always have one rule: when you visit me, you speak the language where I live. I attended her wedding in 2014 in France, and it was an amazing opportunity to continue my French, this time as both speaker and translator for my husband!

During my long weekend with Véronique, we celebrated Epiphany together with her group of friends. We chatted in French over wine, king cake, coffee, cheese, and more wine. In total, I spent four days immersed in the French language and culture. It was a deep dive into the lifestyle and language I longed to master. I picked up slang, mannerisms, and best of all, confidence that I could do this.

It was just what I needed.

I scored in the top level on the entrance exam when I returned to Strasbourg, unlocking the ability to take history, journalism, and politics courses in French. Those who scored lower on the entrance exam were required to choose larger numbers of language classes in their class schedule. I was thrilled to be able to learn in my second language and glean the nuances of French thought on everything from World War II to daily political thought.

It also meant I forged life-long friendships with other Europeans. I became quite close to Verena Vogt, a German au pair studying in Strasbourg, and a pair of journalists, Tamara Theissen and Benoît Fink. Tamara was a Tasmanian travel writer and Benoît was an Alsatian who wrote for the local paper. Benoît went on to hold a lengthy career writing around the world for the French wire service, Agence France-Presse (AFP). Tamara's travel writing, likewise, took her around the world, and she's still doing it—once again from Paris, France.

We spent hours drinking and sharing opinions on life, journalism, and the world as it was. At the time, President Bill Clinton had just launched air assaults in Bosnia. The idea of American bombs anywhere near Europe was alarming. There were also our expatriate observations to be shared and scrutinized. We had enough common English between us that if we needed help with vocabulary to maintain our conversations in French, we could usually find the word or concept. It was just the sort of engagement in local conversation and culture I needed to solidify my ability to think and reason in a second tongue.

But there were downsides to my decision to avoid speaking English during my time in France. First and foremost, it strained my relationships with my English speaking friends. I was studying in Strasbourg at the same time as one of my dearest friends, Elizabeth Goodman. While she chose to live in the college dormitory, I chose to rent a room from a host family. She and I didn't spend as much time together as we could have, in part because of my decision to spend the majority of my time with French speakers. I can imagine it wasn't an easy decision for her to accept. I've always felt regret for how I presented my choice to her and other friends who took a different approach to mastering the language than I did.

I fear I presented myself as an arrogant young woman, and I did little to dispel those conclusions in others. In hindsight, I should have better explained the motivating force behind my decision to preserve those friendships. I'm confident I could have presented this decision with more tact and grace, which admittedly are not my strongest qualities.

▶ LESSON 5

You won't learn another language without speaking it all the time. Loneliness and isolation are effective motivators to learn and master a new language. So, don't only hang out with the expats. Make a decision to spend time with the speakers of the language you are trying to master. They will be far better teachers than any classroom can furnish. And I highly recommend while giving yourself this ultimatum, you have the caveat that you do it with kindness toward those who do not share your conviction.

Chapter 6

NEW YEAR'S EVE SALES JOB

Strasbourg, France

1998–1999

B EFORE LEAVING FOR France, I had filled out paperwork outlining the type of internship I wanted to pursue at the local French television station, France 3 Alsace. Alsace is the French province bordering Germany. Those who live there are called Alsatians. They speak French, German, and a German-sounding French called Alsatian.

Unlike other internships on the list, there wasn't a well-worn path through the doors of France 3. Nonetheless, I arrived expecting everything to be set up. The internship placement director at my study abroad campus was a middle-aged woman with a bureaucratic sensibility. Like most French office workers (particularly in a government town like Strasbourg), she took a lengthy lunch break, left on time, and appeared to have little investment or excitement in the role or duties.

When I inquired about the internship I had imagined, she gave me a blank look and told me in no uncertain terms that, *"Ce n'est pas possible (It's not possible)."*

PICTURED: (L)
Strasbourg, France, 1999.
(R) France 3 newsroom,
Alsace in 1999.

"C'est possible," I fumed to myself. "It is possible." I was determined to prove it to her.

As soon as I learned the biography of one of my professors, his connections to other journalists in Strasbourg, and the seat at the Council of Europe he held, I poured out my sob story of loss and betrayal. I asked him if there was any way he could help me get to know someone at France 3 Alsace, the regional bureau for the national television network.

He mentioned an invitation to a New Year's Eve party for journalists, one which an association was holding after the actual New Year's Eve to make it easier for journalists to attend outside the busy holiday party season. He invited me along.

I'm grateful to this professor and oh, so grateful for all the "liquid courage" served there. Between cocktails and glasses of full-bodied French red wine, I managed to impress upon the chef *d'entreprise* that I should be the first American he allowed to intern at France 3 Alsace. We toasted with champagne, and I floated back to my apartment, vindicated that indeed, *"C'est possible."*

With my typical "grace and tact," I made sure to let the internship coordinator know she, in fact, was wrong. And I would indeed be doing an internship at France 3.

Despite not having college credit for it, I experienced a far better version of a television internship than many of my French peers. While they had to stay behind in the newsroom and write copy for internships that required credit, I was untethered by expectations. I accompanied reporters and photographers on stories throughout Alsace and the neighboring province of Lorraine. This deepened my appreciation for the diversity within France itself.

One of my most influential memories was the day we set off for the Tunnel de Sainte-Marie-aux-Mines. Officially known as le Tunnel Maurice-Lemaire, it lies between Alsace and Lorraine. That spring, a deadly fire in Italy's Mont Blanc Tunnel had claimed 39 lives. A Belgian transport truck carrying flour and margarine caught fire. The driver was unable to get it under control and forced to flee, trapping other vehicles in the tunnel who could not turn around or whose engines stalled with the lack of oxygen. That incident led to a review of tunnel safety throughout France, and we headed for the tunnel to examine its safety for ourselves.

The reporter I was with was either incredibly gracious or perhaps just saw the opportunity to nap on the clock. When we arrived, I volunteered to interview a driver alongside the photographer while we drove through the tunnel. We flagged down a truck, and piled into the noisy cab with a Belgian truck driver whose French was heavily accented and at times difficult for me to understand. But he spoke simply, and I asked simple questions. It was exhilarating to have a conversation with this driver about this event and know it would end up being part of a story on the French evening news. I was over the moon! I couldn't wait to get back to the bureau and write my script. This one definitely went on my French resume tape.

Another key, and much lighter memory was traveling the path of the auto race which came through Alsace province. People were so excited to be able to watch from their own homes and shop windows as the race used the streets through the countryside, rather than a race track. My most vivid memory was the rhyming language the reporter used in his storytelling. I adopted it for mine as well: *"quelques'un pour le tour, d'autres pour le sport...*(Some for the ride, others for the sport)."

These were moments where I felt my grasp of French was truly growing, and my knowledge of its diversity and history was, too. I always tried to go out with the reporters traveling some distance and spent the ride peppering them with questions. We frequently had a leisurely and deliberate sit-down meal for lunch, which gave me more opportunity to pick their brains.

In many ways, this was the highlight of my experience studying abroad and important training for a cub journalist. I am forever grateful that I experienced both the power and high politics of Strasbourg's Council of Europe, while also discovering first-hand Alsace's unique culture outside of Strasbourg.

▶ LESSON 6

Sometimes your vision or concept is out of the comfort zone of the culture you're in. Anticipate this possibility from the outset so you can be prepared for it. Had I considered that this would be a heavy lift for the internship coordinator, I could have avoided my disappointment and bitterness and potentially helped her achieve my objective.

Chapter 7

SVENSKA FLIKA COMES HOME

Sweden

1999

THROUGHOUT MY CHILDHOOD, there were references to the fact that my mother's mom was a "svenska flika" or "a Swedish girl." We called her "Mormor" or "mother's mother." My uncle's kids called her "Farmor" or "father's mother." She came to the United States at age 15, alone, by ship, looking for a new start.

When she first arrived, Mormor lived with her aunt who was a popular seamstress and tailor specializing in knock-off fashion. Mormor later moved to live and work as a child's nurse for a wealthy family in Connecticut.

She met my Italian grandfather on a blind date in New York and the rest is history. They had four children before he passed away in his forties due to Crohn's disease, leaving her to care for the kids on her own. This was a tall order. Her seventh-grade education did not prepare her to support a family, and my grandfather's pension did not offset the financial hardship. But she soldiered on, relying on friends and relatives on the Italian side because she had little to no contact with any Swedish family living in the United States.

PICTURED:
Mormor Siv
Cacamis and I
through the years.

Like many from her generation, she wanted to weave into the fabric of America, not keep her customs or her language. She did not try to teach her children Swedish; she never took them back to the homeland; and she did not visit the homeland herself. My mom recalls that she learned how to make Swedish meatballs from her great-aunt instead of her mother.

For Mormor, there were real reasons to forget her past. There was a lot of pain in her childhood. She was born to a young, unmarried Swedish girl and never knew her father. (We always thought he must have been a sailor. We're still looking for him and his descendants.) Her mother left Sweden to pursue her own dreams in the United States, so Mormor was raised by her grandmother in Sweden with strict, Victorian values. This made her the prude in the room by the time she came of age, let alone by the time she met her own grandchildren.

She, like her mother, came to the United States to start over, making the trip alone on a ship with nothing but the promise of a new life ahead of her. She refused to forgive her mother for leaving her in Sweden and never established a relationship with her. Instead, Mormor folded herself into the customs, food, and culture of her Italian in-laws. She heartily embraced the American dream.

By the time I came on the scene, she was a fairly constant figure. She would visit from New York and later moved to Alabama to be close to three of her children who had settled in Mobile. We saw her for meals and fast-food treats. She always had sweets for us, never let us miss dessert, and frequently made the most mouthwatering Italian meatballs you could eat. Nearly all her cooking was Italian. We rarely had anything Swedish or any discussion of her homeland. She had more of a taste for Italian cookies and cannolis than for the wonders of Swedish gingerbread. She enjoyed cooking and was proud of her results.

She was unfailingly loyal and supportive of our dreams and activities. She often chauffeured us, making sure she attended our games, plays, and concerts, arriving early to get a good seat.

PICTURED: (Top) Anna Kagelind, me, and Sofia Kagelind when they visited New York City. I'm wearing a necklace with a silver Forget-Me-Not flower on it. This is common in Sweden, and it's a flower Mormor always loved. (Bottom) I'm seen here in Oredro, Sweden on a visit with family.

When she followed us to Michigan, I saw her demonstrate more fear and hesitancy toward new things. She rarely greeted a stranger and did not answer her door if she was not expecting company. She screened her calls and seldom made eye contact when she met someone new.

As we grew up, my mother began to look into my grandmother's past and reconnect with some of the more important figures. This included family she located in Michigan. My mom located long-lost aunts, cousins, and those who never left the old country hometown of Karlstad, or the nearby towns of Örebro and Skara.

By the time I was in my early teens, we had regular communication and relationships with these family members. My mother was learning and, in turn, teaching us more of our Swedish heritage, whether it was how we were related to those abroad, or how to make Swedish meatballs or *Pepparkakor* (gingerbread.)

What seemed to help Mormor become more willing to share her culture with us was the arrival of Ikea to the United States. The big blue and yellow box store carried Swedish design, but more importantly, Swedish meals. This was huge for her. She couldn't believe all her favorite foods or her sense of home design was all in one affordable shop. It was where her children and grandchildren wanted to shop. It was a store celebrating everything she'd tried to leave behind. It wasn't until we moved to Pennsylvania that we would make trips for her favorite foods like Lingonberry jam, Swedish meatballs, *glug* mix, and jars of salted or pickled fish or "lutefisk."

As my family grew to know our own generation of cousins who live in Sweden, we planned Mormor's first return. She had never stopped writing a handful of cousins and a dear best friend in Swedish.

But first, I traveled to Örebro, Skara, and Göteborg to see my cousins on my own. I did this during my February break during my study abroad program in France.

I had weathered some pretty cold and snowy winters in Michigan and later at Syracuse University in New York. But the iciness of the

Swedish winter was truly bitter, its intensity stinging my cheeks and piercing through my wool sweaters and warm coats. The snow would come down in sheets. Social life for my cousin in Göteborg was a matter of drifting from apartment to school to bar, always wrapped up tightly and wearing big clunky snow boots. I rarely saw anyone of a different race, certainly no one with dark skin. The most diversity I experienced there was a French friend who was studying in Sweden with my cousin.

My hosts always offered me a welcome gift and constant hospitality, whether it was baked goods or a homemade dinner. We called each other by the Swedish word we'd learned for the closest thing we were to each other, a distant fifth or sixth cousin.

Both of these college-aged women baked and cooked for themselves in ways you would not find the average American college student doing. They were not heating up microwave dinners or ordering midnight pizza—they were baking bread, special rolls, and cookies.

When I traveled to my other cousin's home in Örebro, I received the same warm welcome: a gift upon arrival, lots of baked wonders, and a generous and welcoming attitude.

Friends of mine, with no family in Sweden, say they found their visits to the Nordic country not only cold from a temperature standpoint, but cold relationally as well. They reported difficulty meeting and interacting with people, even though the Swedes spoke excellent English. All of this behavior echoed my growing up experience with Mormor.

When Mormor arrived for Midsummer's Eve (a celebration of nearly 24 hours of sunlight) with my parents and brother in Sweden, it was June 25, 1999. We had plans to reconnect with family members in Stockholm, Skara, and Karlstad.

I'll never forget taking a bike trip with my mom and saying hello to the passersby, who didn't respond or acknowledge our greeting. We initially chalked it up to our being "overly-friendly Americans." But my mom observed it was just like how Mormor behaved toward people not in our family or her small circle of friends. Like her, there was a cautiousness around outsiders here, not the curiosity or openness we would expect in an American or Italian home.

These observations are not to say they are inherently antisocial or negative traits. No, our Swedish family certainly loves to have a good time and celebrate occasions. But caution, being reserved, and yet an amazing sense of domestic capability seemed to characterize them.

From this experience, I learned it's important to not only understand a person in the context where you meet them, but in the context of their family, heritage, and culture.

▶ LESSON 7

Culture doesn't leave people when they leave the culture. Even at a young age, personality traits, habits, and ways of looking at the world are all embedded. That doesn't mean they can't change, but I suspect they have to be consciously identified to be changed.

Chapter 8

YOU NEED YOUR FACE
TO DO YOUR JOB

Afghanistan
Summer, 2009

❝ JESSICA, YOU NEED YOUR face to do your job," said my dad.

It was the summer of 2009. I had spent the first six months of the year looking for work after the economy crashed, leaving my national and regional newsroom clients with little to no margin to hire freelancers. While it began out of desperation, my decision to plan a reporting trip to Afghanistan and cover the war build-up and national elections was a firm one.

With a new president in the White House, and a war that had outlasted the president who started it, the timing was good. There would be a story, and few networks had people in position to cover it. On top of a national election for Afghanistan, President Obama would request an assessment of whether the conflict international partners and American troops had been fighting could be won.

My trip was inspired by a chance lunch I'd had with a former local news colleague, Conor Powell. We briefly crossed paths when I freelanced at the Washington D.C. ABC affiliate where he worked at the time. He told me he was getting gear together to go to Afghanistan and freelance produce, report, shoot—whatever he could. I told him he was crazy. But the conversation stuck with me as did the idea. Why shouldn't I try to do the same thing?

My dad had a very quick response to that question. "We're not just talking about dying," he said. "What if you live but you're seriously wounded? Maimed? Burned? Will this still be the right decision then?" My dad isn't known for shock-value, so his words made a big impression on me. But he had taught me to make decisions methodically. I had done a lot of research and preparation. And prayed.

One day, I was reading in Ruth 2:8: "So Boaz said to Ruth, "My daughter, listen to me. Don't go and glean in another field and don't go away from here." Suddenly, it was clear to me. Journalism is my field, my calling, I thought. God doesn't want me to leave it.

The first bit of confirmation came with a connection to Abbas Daiyar, a young man who would become my fixer, translator, and friend. A fixer is someone who arranges shelter, transportation, meals, technology, security, and anything else required for another person. Journalists and aid workers often use fixers to parachute into a new country or location.

I learned of Abbas Daiyar through an editor at *FOXNews.com*. Abbas had taught his peers English in the camps in Pakistan. One of those students was Ahmad Shuja, a young Afghan intern at *FOXNews.com*. Abbas was already a working journalist in Afghanistan. An ethnic Hazara, his background allowed the most contact with Western women, a looser version of Shia Islam, and he seemed to possess more critical thinking than some of the Pashtun men I met in Afghanistan (Pashtun is the dominant ethnicity in Afghanistan). All of this was favorable to creating a working relationship.

My first call to Abbas was nerve-wracking. What would he be like? How could I figure out at this distance whether he was trustworthy? I had to make a judgement call without meeting him in person. I had to take a chance.

We discussed story ideas, safety precautions, what he could help me with (a guest house, a driver) and what he could not (access to military bases, transportation to Bagram Air base, transportation to the more dangerous or what the military calls "kinetic" areas of the country).

I tried to ask questions I could verify the answers to independently. By then, I had read a great deal about the Afghan tribes and customs, and I tried to gauge his perspective in comparison to the attributes I had read about. Still, like the decision to go to Afghanistan in the first place, hiring Abbas was largely a step of faith.

In the days that followed, my decision was confirmed as pieces I could never have put into place just came together. When that happens, particularly after I've committed a decision to prayer, I take it as a green light to go full throttle ahead, pending any red or yellow flags.

I continued to spread the word about my plans, and people throughout my personal network began to step forward with ideas, resources, connections, and even equipment. Someone told me about an outlet which would sponsor freelance journalists for a military embed. (This is the term for when a journalist is attached to a military unit during a conflict. In exchange for food, shelter and some level of protection, the journalist receives access to the troops, and their commanders for the purposes of covering the conflict.) Finding that sponsor proved critical because the military requires you to write down an affiliation or outlet when you apply for an embed. The Pentagon wants to know to whom it's granting an audience.

My housemate had a friend who was dating a member of Army Special Forces. The boyfriend gave me a used helmet, a retired flak jacket, and lent me a pair of backpacks and other critical survival gear.

PICTURED: Me and my dad pose before I board my flight to India en route to Afghanistan in 2009.

Someone else told me about a foundation which awarded financial scholarships to freelance journalists seeking to undergo Hostile Environment & Emergency First-Aid training. Attending the instructional session gave me confidence that I could administer some basic first-aid and identify some types of weapons and the corresponding sounds they make when fired. On a practical level, completing the training guaranteed me a lower rate on travel insurance. It also put me in touch with well-respected journalists who I worked with years later at the White House.

I consulted with fellow photographers to design a system of photography, videography, audio-gathering, and editing gear at reasonable prices. They advised me on the types of equipment which could weather rough terrain and treatment, and how to transmit sound and video via a satellite system I could rent called a *BGAN*.

Friends, and eventually even my dad, kicked in their contacts as well. My dad's medical school pal was serving in the army reserves as a physician and helped me find someone to drive me to my military embed which began at Bagram Air Base. One of my high school best friends put me in touch with someone who lent me head scarves and told me where to buy a copy of the Muslim holy book called the Qu'ran and a *salwar kameez*, the typical garb of women in Afghanistan.

All the while, Abbas and I were developing story ideas I could pitch to newspapers, radio networks, television, whatever and whomever I could convince to take my work.

By June, I began cold-calling news outlets. I told them I planned to cover the upcoming elections and the security assessment and would be in Afghanistan on my own dime. "I'll be there anyway, and I'm working on the following stories," I would say. "Are you interested in any of these ideas?"

Then, I called *FOX News Radio*. Hank Weinbloom picked up the phone. "Don't go just for us," I recall him saying in a fatherly tone. "I don't know how much work we will take."

"I'm not," I reassured him, not even knowing at the time who else would become my client.

It paid $50.00 for each 30 second report, not even close to making the risk financially worth it. But the ability to work for a national radio network on this adventure proved priceless, and it drove me forward. It was one of a series of big breaks for which I've always been grateful.

I also phoned up editors and managers at *USA Today*, *The Washington Times*, *The Catholic News Service*, *FoxNews.com*, a collection of old and new media which didn't make any sense to someone else from the outside. But they made sense to me because each of them came through relationships, and each required me to adapt to a different type of media. This is a critical ingredient for success in journalism, or any career, and essential for a freelancer who is traveling on spec hoping to cover the cost of the trip with money earned from her coverage.

I would later teach other journalists how to self-finance their trips and to sell their work once they got to their destination, or after they returned. For example, I could take video and audio of everything I experienced and return back to my cot with raw material. I could spin this into an online article, or a 30-second radio spot, or sell the video to a television network—or all three.

Print reporters record everything for accuracy. But I had to adapt quickly and assess whether a story was a better fit for a certain medium. That interview with a general could be a radio spot, but then quotes from it could spur on a new print story or give me content for an existing one.

All these incredibly important skills have since served me well. Whether I traveled on my dime or flew business class all expenses paid, the need to adapt to changing logistics, language, personality, and personnel was never far away. What's more, it likely prepared me for the constant reality that the very act of journalism has changed drastically during my career.

After all, I was not tweeting from Kabul or base camp in those days.

▶ LESSON 8

When you're preparing to enter a new culture or country, know everyone already in your life is a resource. Include them in your dream, and you will build a movement that makes them want to help.

Secondly, share your path with others. For years after I made this trip, I shared my experience with others who wanted to do the same. I spoke at journalism conferences, met for coffee with journalists and aid workers who wanted to cover or help in Afghanistan. This is part of building a network. As the world becomes more interconnected, the chances increase that someone in, or connected to your network, will have the answers you seek.

Chapter 9

GO TIME

Afghanistan
Summer, 2009

I'LL NEVER FORGET THE lump in my throat and the tightness in my chest as I walked off the airplane into the thick, dusty Kabul air. I was wearing a *salwar kameez* over hiking clothes, my blonde hair covered with a head scarf and hiking boots peeking out, sweat pouring down my back.

There was no way I blended in. I looked absolutely ridiculous.

Abbas Daiyar was there to meet me. No cars were permitted to pick up at the terminal, so I walked toward the parking lots where we'd agreed to meet. I'd only seen a photo of his face, but unlike me, he didn't have to hide it. He was slight, dressed in western garb and had a new cell phone and calling cards already pre-purchased for me. He looked just like his picture, and he'd already laid out money on my behalf. All of these facts were very good signs.

We told some amazing stories on that trip, beginning in Kabul with election preparations. Then there was a trip to the famous Buddhas of

Bamiyan, and even further north to the Band-e-Amir National Park of Afghanistan, which had received hundreds of thousands of dollars of United States taxpayer money for tourism even though it was completely inaccessible to Western visitors.

I remember downloading video from that day via an electricity converter run off the car battery as we bounced wildly along the rock-studded road. By the time we arrived back at our guest house, I felt as though I'd ridden a bucking bronco in a rodeo.

Bamiyan was like taking a trip back in time. The Afghans gathered brush to burn for fuel and heat; they grew their own food and stored it in caves to keep it cool; and they fashioned goat milk into dried balls to gnaw on for calcium during the harsh winter months. There were no luxuries such as toilets, electricity, or running water. But this was the heartland for the Hazara people, the one province where they formed the majority ethnicity. And at the time, it was orders of magnitude safer than the rest of the country. We didn't require security to move about the province.

Abbas and I had written dozens of emails prior to meeting, but the true moments of cultural enlightenment happened gathered around food after a day of discovery and reporting. One night, Abbas and other Hazaras shared stories of the persecution their people had endured at the hands of the Taliban. They were rounded up and massacred like the Jews during World War II. They had read about the Jewish Zionist movement, the search for a state based on ethnicity and religion. They yearned to have the same type of state—free from persecution. Their brand of Shia Islam had mixed with the rituals of Buddhism, the religion they repeatedly adopted when not being forcibly converted by successive waves of nomadic Muslim conquerors.

I sat there struck by the irony of the situation. I had come to a Muslim country, from which fundamentalist radicals attacked my country, where American troops fought the influence of the Taliban, and yet this is where I find Muslims who can't wait to talk to me because of my Jewish heritage? I never admitted I had any Jewish heritage to most of the people I interacted with in Afghanistan! I felt it was too dangerous. But in this conversation, I found myself wishing I knew more of my relatives who had traveled back to Israel, currently lived in communes called *kibbutzim*, and served in the Israeli military. In some ways, that would have deepened a connection I didn't expect to discover. Despite all my efforts to understand their culture, they were just as interested in understanding mine.

Abbas and I toured through the caves behind the famous Buddhas of Bamiyan which are UNESCO world heritage sites. The guide told us of the Taliban having strapped bombs to the Hazara people in 2001 and lashing them to the face of these ancient Buddhas carved into the foothills of the Himalayas. With one push of a button, innocent human lives were eviscerated, and the history and significance of these 6th century ancient carvings was taken from a proud minority population.

We saw footprints on the ceiling of some of the caves said to be from the Taliban throwing their shoes at the roof in a sign of disrespect. At the bottom of the cliffs stood a few cages made of chicken wire and wood which held the broken pieces of the Buddhas, saved just in case the world did in fact successfully raise the millions of dollars needed to restore these sites. It's been more than 10 years, and the work has not moved forward tangibly.

That was the most peaceful part of the trip.

The rest of my time in Afghanistan was spent adapting to another new culture: the United States military. I embedded with the United States Army's 10th Mountain Division and their attached special forces unit. It's an institution based on rules, routine, and a top-down chain

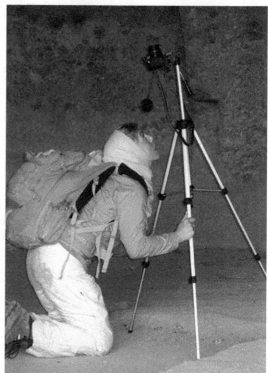

PICTURED:
(Top-R) Bamiyan
Province, Afghanistan.
(Bottom) Abbas Daiyar
& me in Band-e-Amir,
Afghanistan 2009.

PICTURED:
(Top) Me photographing the majestic sapphire blue lakes of Band-e-Amir. (Bottom) Bamiyan Province, Afghanistan.

PICTURED: (Top-L) When I saw this picture of Sergeant First Class Chet Millard on the cover of *Time Magazine,* I thought he was dead. We spent 14 hours together in a military convoy in Afghanistan. Fortunately, I learned he is still alive. (Top-R) A female shura a in 2009 in Wardak Province, Afghanistan. (Bottom-L) A female voter casts her ballot in the 2009 presidential election. (Bottom-R) General Stanley McChrystal sits with Wardak Province Governor, Halim Fidai, and local police officials during his 2009 assessment of Operation Enduring Freedom in Afghanistan.

of command. (Remember how much I loved those qualities in my Alabama experience?) In addition, my experience learning how to decipher the truth and the context around it was incredibly challenging.

In the background for all of us lay the emotional stress of knowing death was never far away, even when we didn't witness it. I was eating lunch with the brigade commander hours after we got the news that a well-known American female reporter had been severely injured when her convoy was attacked. The colonel was visibly shaken coming back from the operating tent. I'm grateful to say she's back on the job and as tenacious as ever.

On another occasion, I rode in a helicopter to a funeral ceremony at an outpost for a young U.S. soldier who had been killed. The colonel and I peered over the side and watched an attack on other soldiers also on their way. The staff sergeant I'd eaten lunch with was in the vehicle. He lost his legs. Others lost their lives.

There was a harrowing drive with a route clearing crew whose sole job was to locate and disarm roadside bombs and IEDs to protect the troops who came behind. They served in the Wisconsin National Guard and seemed grateful for the company of a woman, swapping stories and interested in what they did. At one point, we stopped and there was an exchange of gunfire outside the vehicle.

I peeked my head out of the gunner's slot to get photos, and they pulled me back in. Later, the convoy was hit. No deaths, but at least one interpreter was injured. They were a young group led by a wizened soldier. They shared stories of the jobs and families and communities left behind to serve in Afghanistan as national guards. The leader would later be on the front-page photo of a *Time Magazine* in my mailbox when I returned to the United States, his eyes closed, a cigarette in his mouth. It nearly gave me a heart attack thinking he was dead until I read the article to discover he survived.

There was also the time I got dehydrated and lightheaded on an early morning mountain climb with some troops in the Logar Valley.

Unfortunately, I became a burden to them, not a removed observer, when they had to escort me back to our camp and fashion a saline drip into my arm. That was a super emotionally wretched moment for me as I knew I had put them in danger because my body hadn't properly adjusted to the mountain heights. I felt horrible physically and emotionally.

While I was covering violence, strategy, and war, I was also writing about the Catholic community in Afghanistan. *The Catholic News Service* was an excellent client (the only one who volunteered additional pay due to the dangers I faced) through whom I met the priest at the lone Christian church in Kabul located on the Italian embassy grounds. He gave regular mass to a very small group of the occasional embassy staffer and the nuns. The nuns had a ministry to children, meeting their physical needs while not being able to discuss the reason which motivated their service. It's illegal to evangelize in Afghanistan.

I was able to explore the chaplain shortage issue and feed my own soul through meaningful and encouraging conversations with clergy and soldiers. When death is never far from you, spiritual matters come up more regularly in conversation. As a person with a strong personal faith, I sure needed the outlet and comfort of seeing all of the pain and suffering around me in light of a bigger, broader plan—something fashioned by the hands of a loving and powerful God who could somehow redeem it. I never could have conquered the inherent fears of going to a war zone without being a follower of Jesus. I had to be confident that if it was my time to go, I was ready to meet my Maker.

Election Day tested me differently. I spent my time chasing mortars for images as they rained down on polling locations. Voters were streaming in. I doubled back to talk to them for my stories. It was a very insecure election process. Simple paper ballots stuffed in Rubbermaid containers. No computers.

No security measures were in place, save the purple ink-died thumb as a means of avoiding repeat voters. I don't think I fully processed how incredibly dangerous it was to chase after bombs until many months afterwards. And yet it was part of the story, the story I was there to tell.

And there was the day General Stanley McChrystal arrived in Wardak Province to work on his assessment for the president. I first heard the news as soldiers excitedly shared it among themselves. It was the main military headline of my time there, and it was coming to me. President Barack Obama had ordered a new assessment of the progress, or lack thereof, in order to decide whether to draw down or surge additional troops into Afghanistan. McChrystal was touring the country to conduct that process, interviewing community members, leaders, and coalition soldiers on what was and wasn't working in their counter insurgency strategy.

Despite being told he would likely not answer my questions, I climbed aboard the transport to where he was meeting in a mini-shura with community leaders and members. A shura is a consultative meeting. There, I met Lieutenant General Michael Flynn and his brother Charlie, both high ranking officers in the United States Army.

Michael Flynn was a key member of McChrystal's inner circle. Flynn had followed McChrystal to Afghanistan as the key officer in charge of collecting intelligence. He was to apply it to a counterinsurgency strategy both felt was successful in Iraq and now being deployed in Afghanistan. Only later would Flynn face prison time for allegedly advancing foreign policy for President Donald Trump before he was installed in office, a violation of the Hatch Act.

I was there as McChrystal sat down with community leaders to listen as they described their security needs and capabilities to meet them. While I wasn't approved to do a one-on-one interview with McChrystal, I hustled to keep up with him and the high-level officers. They toured around a wooded hill, with Afghan security on one side and American security on the other. I rolled video (we didn't have much footage of McChrystal at the time, so I knew it would be valuable) and captured audio as McChrystal held conversations with Afghan politicians, community leaders, and police officers. The conversations he had in my hearing provided enough information to write articles and radio hits as well as sell video of his assessment process throughout the day.

I was a sweaty, heavy-breathing journalist as I snapped a picture (*page 79*) of the general listening intently as the Afghan police described the security situation in Logar Province.

What I recall most about that day is witnessing a man of action and decisiveness being truly present as a student. General McChrystal demonstrated the art of observation that is so paramount when two differing cultures come together. He listened intently, asked follow-up questions, made notes, and appeared genuinely interested in what he was being told. Looking back, I wonder how he came to the conclusion that surging foreign troops into the country could change the course of generations of tribal conflict and insecurity. The presidential decisions which emerged from his assessment neglected to end the United States military operation in Afghanistan. Instead, they only deepened it.

Another day, a group of social scientists, embedded in the military to help soldiers understand the psychology of the communities they were working in, arranged an all-female *shura*. This *shura* was to gather additional intelligence from the Afghan women, who, while culturally sidelined, often heard information useful to uncovering plots against coalition soldiers and other "enemies." According to custom, it had to be sponsored by a man in the community who would open his home and his protection to a group of women.

There were women who spoke only Pashto—the dominant language—and those who spoke only Farsi. The organizers had translators for all of them. These women brought their daughters and sons. Once inside the plaza, their culture allowed them to dress as they did inside their own homes. Off came the burkas and the drab coverings to reveal bright, gauzy silks in a rainbow of colors, piercings and gold jewelry, tattoos, and hennaed hair glowing a range of red and strawberry blonde in the harsh sunlight.

My emotions swelled and my eyes filled with tears. I was with more women than I had seen in more than a month. I hadn't realized how much I was missing female companionship. Despite not being able to communicate, just the presence and sameness brought comfort.

The sociologists divided the women into smaller, language-based groups. I listened as they asked questions about the women's community, health, sense of safety, and use of technology. This led us to a fascinating discovery.

Even after the Taliban was driven from government, it was still customary to marry off very young women to men selected by their fathers. Frequently, these girls met their husbands the day of their wedding. But the introduction of small, cheap mobile phones into the community allowed the girls to secretly text their betrothed, giving them at least some meaningful control over getting to know their future spouses.

While they still lacked the cultural equity to marry for love, this small technological advance meant they didn't have to marry a complete stranger.

▶ LESSON 9

Take time to listen. You have two ears and one mouth for a reason! Before you form your own conclusion, test those perspectives against other available information. Don't consider your own perspective superior.

You'll also learn that every culture has assumptions, stereotypes, and blind spots. During this trip, the Hazara saw every political decision in Afghanistan as motivated by ethnic discrimination. Likewise, the United States Army often saw their decisions as superior to the Afghan leaders who relied on additional factors that would never occur to Western minds.

Chapter 10

PARACHUTING IN TO CHAOS

Port-au-Prince, Haiti

March 2010

THE DEVASTATING PICTURES OF the January 12, 2010, Haiti earthquake haunted me. Nearly a quarter of a million people died. Because the epicenter was so close to populated areas, more than one million people were left homeless. My television was filled with pictures of rubble which had once housed thousands, those who had already been living on the brink of starvation and economic collapse.

While I had never been to Haiti, my Francophone leanings gave me an affinity for all former French colonies. Plus, having returned from Afghanistan, I now had a taste for parachuting into chaos. I had to be in the middle of the action. But responding to a natural catastrophe means you must have a plan to get on the ground and the backing and equipment to get there. It's much harder as a solo-journalist to make that move. I didn't have months to plan a trip like I did before traveling to Afghanistan.

Three weeks later, I was invited by a church friend to the Washington, D.C. National Prayer Breakfast. The annual president's National

Prayer Breakfast is a non-denominational event hosted by Congress to provide a time for reflection, prayer and inspiration around the teachings of Jesus of Nazareth, which draws men and women from all countries and all walks of life each year to the Nation's Capital. Many people meet for the first time across all kinds of boundaries and form long-lasting bonds of friendship.

With the obvious needs in Haiti, the prayer breakfast gave extra focus on how to help in its recovery. It was the perfect opportunity to meet leaders of these aid groups and enlist their help to getting in Haiti.

I collected a lot of business cards and came home confident I could travel to Haiti with their help. I also learned the United Nations would hold a donor conference at the end of March to collect pledges toward rebuilding Haiti the already impoverished country.

I set about planning live coverage of the donor conference from Port-au-Prince. A week-long trip would give me an opportunity to demonstrate the need for the donations ahead of the conference and get some reporting material for other clients. I approached *FOX News Radio* with the idea to do live two-ways for three mornings around the conference, and offer other radio vignettes. The great part of commercial radio is that they're 30-second stories. You can do multiple versions of the stories for another client and get the companies to share costs.).

An aid organization called World Relief was my resource for finding a guest house. These are typically places where non-governmental organizations (NGOs) house their volunteers. A guest house would give me a chance to stay at little to no cost, plus provide the benefit of regular access to volunteers who were serving in places where I was not. That could help generate more leads for stories.

I soon realized the treasure trove of information these aid workers could provide. They were well-connected to other aid groups; they knew where the problem spots were in the response; and they had government connections.

Throughout my week there, I worked with a variety of agencies from Catholic Relief Services, World Vision, World Relief, Compassion International, and other non-religious aid groups like CHF, an international development and humanitarian assistance organization, which now goes by the name, Global Communities.

Since French is still taught in Haiti and spoken by the elites and political class, my French was helpful in navigating parts of the fact-finding phase. My knowledge of the military was also helpful. By then, United States Southern Command, the part of the American military responsible for South and Central America as well as the Caribbean, had organized a tremendous response of food and supplies to bring into the country. I worked through those contacts to plan interviews with their leadership and to understand how and where they were organizing their efforts.

I requested to embed with the United States Army units engaged in the response to cover what they were doing—just as I had in Afghanistan, but they were offering no embeds. Nonetheless, they were definitely part of the unfolding story there. I did one story on the Navy "Seabees," the engineers who worked on setting up camps for displaced persons. Many soldiers were also working to ensure safety at the camps where desperate people were housed beneath tarps, one makeshift shelter right on top of the next.

As Haiti is predominantly Catholic, I covered the first Easter post-earthquake. *The Catholic News Service* had taken many articles from Afghanistan and was interested in coverage of Good Friday and Easter services in Haiti.

The flight to Port-au-Prince was short and full of aid workers and Haitian businesspeople. One told me of the lawlessness his family had experienced under the dictators who ran Haiti from the 1950s through

PICTURED:

(L) Interviewing a United States solider in charge of dispersing supplies to Haiti after the 2010 earthquake. (Top-L) A main street in Port-au-Prince is filled with rubble as people try to return to daily life. March 2010. (Middle-L) Cathedral of Our Lady of Assumption, Easter Sunday, 2010. (Middle) Easter Mass, March 2010. (Bottom-R) After the 2010 earthquake, many children were dropped off at orphanages because their parents could no longer care for them.

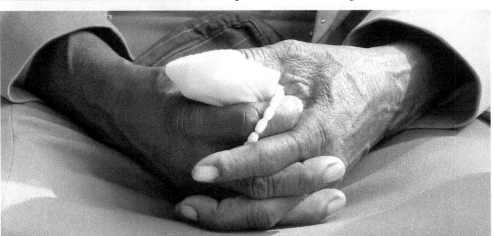

the 1980s. He described having done all his Christmas shopping for his family one year only to have a machete-wielding police force storm his compound. They demanded the presents for their own families at knife-point. He worried that the country would descend into further chaos with thousands of people newly homeless and safe food and water now more scarce than ever.

I stepped into the airport and into a hot, wet, wall of air. Even in March, the sun beat down unremittingly. I had not yet worked anywhere this hot and humid. I arrived with a head cold, but I could still smell my own odor mixed with dust. My planning had to include time of day, heat, and constant access to bottled water, something we all competed over.

That week, I worked closely with a wonderful man named Elie Lafortune. He had been the Country Director for World Relief in the Republic of Congo. He returned to his native Haiti to work on economic development and relief and set up micro-entrepreneurship and other financial instruments to help lift people out of poverty. Elie was completely overqualified to work as a fixer, but he was willing to help me because of relationships we both had with people in World Relief. Elie helped me plan those days and scout interview locations. He used his relationships for stories with over-worked and under-appreciated aid workers who were mired in the debris of an already crumbling city.

Elie had a warm smile, a keen sense of what made a good story, and he spoke excellent French, English, and Creole. One of the best moments of the trip was when I introduced Elie to an ambassador, giving him a connection worth way more than any payment I could give him for his help.

Just as I shared in Lesson 8, I relied on personal connections with NGOs, staying a few nights with Missionary Aviation Fellowship who knew friends of mine. Missionary Aviation Fellowship flies supplies to remote missionaries. I interviewed the Mennonite Central Committee engineers who were evaluating what structures could be saved (my mom taught at a Mennonite School), and interviewed children and instructors at a Compassion International camp in Carrefour. In this camp, students studied and received meals amid the devastation. I have sponsored children in these types of camps through Compassion International since I was 14. With just a small sum of monthly support, they receive food, education, and religious instruction. I've now had the joy to watch three young people grow and develop knowing I was able to be part of that process.

The people of Haiti can be warm and disarming. As a country whose economy has been dependent on foreign aid, they are accustomed to foreigners visiting. But that didn't mean the color of those foreigners didn't matter. As a white, blonde woman traveling alone, I was grateful Elie was at my side. I was even more grateful others I trusted had vouched for his integrity. It was evident from the moment I arrived that I was in safe hands. Even the men he'd hired to drive us around could make me feel uncomfortable with a glance. There were many men who gave off the impression that they could and would be more aggressive if given the chance.

It was often critical to our access and my safety that Elie remained with me at all times as there were reports of rampant physical and sexual abuse in the camps of displaced people. It's important to remember that when humans are desperate, and these people were incredibly desperate for good reason, they can be extremely dangerous.

Over the week, I accompanied army generals on tours of displacement camps which had taken over the main golf courses in Port-au-Prince; I met volunteers transporting clean water on motorbikes to families living beneath tarps; I met a poet who slept standing so the rest of his family could be more comfortable beneath their tarp-fashioned tent across from the government palace. I interviewed ambassadors, local politicians, witnessed the work of one Hollywood movie star (Sean Penn), and many extraordinary people making the best of a terrible situation.

On Good Friday and Easter Sunday, I visited the historic cathedral in downtown Port-au Prince. For more than 100 years, the Cathedral of Our Lady of Assumption stood as a landmark and as a lighthouse to ships in the Caribbean. In an instant, it had been decimated by the earthquake. Its roof and towers flanking the main entrance collapsed. Archbishop Joseph Serge Miot died instantly. The Vicar General of Port-au-Prince, Monsignor Charles Benoit, was buried alive beneath rubble.

It was a deeply moving experience to interview the faithful on the holiest weekend of the Christian calendar. For them, the holiday was a tangible expression of hope and renewal for their city. I remember the sun coming up over the rose-colored fragments of the cathedral as a crowd, all dressed up for mass, sat beneath a white canopy on the plaza. One elderly grandmother, clad in a bright blue dress, held her white rosary beads in her weathered hands while silently clinging to her faith and willing the words of the priest to encourage her heart.

The loss these people felt was heartbreaking. A third of the 150 member choir perished in the earthquake. One choral singer told me she'd lost all three of her children. And yet, on Easter Sunday, the priest pointed them towards hope, strength, and resilience.

In 2014, Segundo Cardona, the Puerto Rican architect who designed a new cathedral, attended the installation and consecration of a temporary building known as the Transitory Cathedral. In Haiti, often anything designated as temporary becomes permanent.

▶ LESSON 10

Aid workers who work long-term in a country are a natural resource to help you get to know a new community. You can rely on them in-country or out of country. They have already sought answers to many of the same questions you will ask—and formed the relationships to answer them. They can also help expedite your efforts to get into the area.

Just remember, aid workers offer one puzzle piece, not the whole picture. Be aware they have their own biases and preconceptions of the area. Test everything they tell you, just as you would anyone else.

Chapter 11

SLOW RIDE TO BRASILIA

Rio de Janeiro, Brazil

March 2011

❝ YOU WANT ME TO cover President Obama's upcoming trip to
Brazil?" I asked my boss excitedly. That sounds amazing!

It was the spring of 2011. I'd been covering President Barack Obama for *China Central Television* (CCTV) for several months. President
Obama was making a tour of South and Central America to increase
trade ties, warn Brazil and Chile about relying too heavily on China
as a trading partner, and discuss ways the United States could help El
Salvador and Nicaragua with the scourge of drug violence. My boss and
I would need to settle the logistics to get me there, meet a live truck
operator, and do live reports on this visit while trying to shoot some
additional stories on Brazilian-Chinese ties.

Adding to the complexity, Obama spent part of Saturday, March 19,
in Brasilia, and then Sunday, March 20, in Rio de Janeiro. To save costs,
I would not be on the press charter following the president, but taking
commercial flights to do my best to copy this itinerary. We planned for
me to stay at the press hotel in Rio before and after the day in Brasilia,
flying back and forth on the day President Obama began his state visit.

PICTURED: (Top) Barra Beach, Brazil, 2011. (Bottom) Me posing with the *Dragones de Independence,* the guards at the presidential palace in Brasilia.

The hotel was a beautiful, bright, and sparkling luxury resort hotel on Barra da Tijuca. This is a beach about 21 miles from the domestic airport and about 19 miles away from the international airport. But while the distance and travel time seemed short on Google Maps, it would prove to be far longer in practice.

While the hotel's location allowed visitors to stay out of the way of Rio's slums and Copacabana Beach's crowds, it added extra travel for live presentations and reporting. I was often asked to do live shots more than an hour from the hotel. It was a long car ride for just a few minutes of air time. Everything felt longer and more arduous. The heat takes a toll when you're not used to it.

I finally had a break Friday morning to enjoy a couple of hours on the beach. The rest of the day would be a travel day. All I had to do was make a domestic flight to Brasilia that afternoon. The sun's heat was intense as I settled on the beach. Before long, I realized my sunscreen was no match for this intensity. My fair skin was sizzling. I'm not sure if I fell asleep or got lulled into wonder at the beauty around me, but before I knew it, I was running behind.

Having discussed my travel plans with the concierge, I had given myself an hour and a half to get to the domestic airport, more than enough time to travel a distance which according to the maps should take me half that time. I checked out of the hotel and jumped into a taxi to get to the airport.

But it was Friday afternoon. All of Rio was headed out to the beaches. It was the worst traffic I had ever seen. My heart sank. I was now trapped in a car with a non-English speaking taxi driver. I had to make that flight. It was the last one on that airline to Brasilia on Friday, the only one which allowed me to be there in advance of the president's visit.

I was hot. Hot from the lack of air-conditioning, from the sunburn all over my chest and arms, from the shame of missing a flight I should have been able to catch, from the angry tears and frustration, adding more pressure to a high-pressure situation I was facing alone.

When we finally arrived, the flight had already departed. I frantically pulled out my huge suitcases and camera gear from the taxi and paid the cab driver the exorbitant bill from sitting in traffic with a meter running. I hoped to get help from the airline ticket agents.

This was mistake number two. I approached the counter with tears in my eyes and explained my problem in English. The agent said something in Portuguese, shaking her head no. Wait, what? She works in the airline industry and she doesn't speak English? But I had failed to realize a critical distinction—this was an airport with domestic flights only. These airline workers didn't need to speak English.

Brazil is an incredibly large country, the only Portuguese-speaking nation on a continent of Spanish speakers. If Brazilians are going to speak another language, it's probably going to be Spanish. Unlike other trips where I'd brought a phrase book to aid in getting around, it was buried in my luggage and useless to me in my hour of need.

I walked from counter to counter, laden with all my heavy equipment, begging someone to help me get to Brasilia as soon as possible. "Brasilia?" I would inquire. I mixed fragments of French, Spanish, Italian, and English together as I would try to negotiate what I needed.

Finally, I called my boss back in the United States to get some help. Maybe he could find a flight which would get me there, and I could just walk to the counter, put down my credit card and say, "Brasilia?"

Eventually, he found a flight to Brasilia on the airline GO. Now, I had to wait the hours until it would depart, putting me into Brasilia by midnight. I was so relieved, I cried.

The next day I would be covering a state visit with an intense sunburn and on just a couple of hours of sleep.

▶ LESSON 11

Many other countries divide their services between an airport for international flights and one for domestic flights only. At the latter, expect the standard of service for foreign travelers to be much lower. If I had it to do over again, I would have ensured my phrase book was easily-accessible, that I had at least one backup plan if I missed the first flight, and I also should have given myself more time.

Chapter 12

CHINA DOLL

Washington, D.C.

Fall, 2011

I SPENT SEVEN YEARS on staff as a Washington Correspondent and later a White House Correspondent for *China Central Television*, the state broadcaster. I studied no Chinese culture or Chinese management ethos before taking the job. I walked in knowing how to do my job, but knowing little about the cross-cultural currents I was wading into. I wish now I had done so. *CCTV America* took a chance on me. I took a chance on them. While it proved to be a fruitful ride for both of us, I would argue it could have been smoother if I had been more prepared for the cultural differences I encountered.

As their reporter, I had the sole opportunity to learn the Chinese culture and perspective from the inside out while taking unbelievable trips around the world. They, in turn, had a Western face and credible Washington journalist to communicate a Chinese perspective. In Chinese parlance, that was a win-win.

From the beginning, we were navigating layers of differences from the definition of journalism to how to communicate cross-culturally. In the United States, journalism is a profession with ethical and

PICTURED: Preparing to anchor for *CGTN America*'s flagship business show.

moral guidelines, while in China, it's a tool of government communications. Add to that—a whole separate approach to interpersonal communication.

The Westerners, me included, would openly debate, differ, and often loudly discuss our disagreements. For our Chinese colleagues, these mannerisms were deemed aggressive and counterproductive. The absence of debate made it more challenging to reach solutions everyone felt good about.

Furthermore, we Westerners[1] could move on from our differences. But for our Chinese colleagues, there was a mental record of wrongs. Our managers kept a personnel file on each one of the non-Chinese, and it was filled with a log of our actions and infractions.

From the beginning, everything was much harder. The bosses in Beijing thought they could send a bureau in a box—extra copies of their software, their computers, their workflows to Washington, D.C.—and it would just instantly make a working bureau.

Nothing could be farther from the truth. The teleprompters and computers were formatted to work with Chinese characters, not English words. Access to wire services? Nope. We had to aggregate news found on the Internet from reputable sources. Western-trained journalists knew what to look for. Our Chinese colleagues eventually pointed us to what they considered "reliable" Chinese sources of information.

Storing video? No way to do that. We had to rely on Beijing to send us clips from video partners in our hemisphere on a 13-hour time delay. This made it impossible to produce any breaking news.

The editing computers would erase anything we tried to store within three to seven days, depending on how much we were trying to store. It took years before we had our own relationships with video providers like the *Associated Press*, Reuters, NBC, and CNN so we could order video and use it to cover breaking stories.

---

1 https://www.youtube.com/watch?v=e9URH-Ga7_U

Editing video? We had a Chinese system with a manual written in Chinese, and no one could really explain to our show editors how to use it because the only Chinese technicians were engineers, not video editors.

Stylebook? Guidebook? Common standards for attribution, sourcing, how to define our audience? What kinds of stories they wanted to see? Nope.

If Chinese money paid for that bureau, it was American and European ingenuity which brought it to life—fits, tears, screaming matches, and all. Somehow, when I saw the attention to detail for our shiny new set, our control room, and our office space, I really thought it would be a smooth, professional operation out of the gate.

We Westerners were pioneers there to teach our Chinese colleagues. They didn't want to feel like they didn't know what they were doing, even though they didn't. In reality, we, too, were ill-prepared for what we faced. Otherwise, I'm not sure we would have signed up for the job.

I don't think most of the Western journalists the Beijing office hired had worked so hard just to produce 30 minutes of news. Maybe that's why our first 30-minute broadcast in 2011 felt like we'd just given birth, because we had.

▶ LESSON 12

What works in one culture does not necessarily work in another. Yet, we often try to cut and paste across cultures. Whether it's a workflow or a management approach, identify the goal and discuss how you would approach the problem. Then adapt those solutions into a new one which is culturally appropriate for the group. And give yourself extra time and patience... you'll need it.

Chapter 13

MIRACLES AT THE
CHINESE EMBASSY

Washington, D.C

September, 2017

AFTER LAYING THE GROUNDWORK for months to go with President Trump to China for his first state visit, I made a formal proposal to my bosses at *CGTN America* (the now rebranded *CCTV America*). But my passport was already at the Chinese embassy for a different trip under a tourist visa application. One manager worried I could not withdraw it and reapply for a journalism visa to go on a different trip. The top boss said she could work it out and said she wanted me to go.

I began planning the trip with a photographer. We had already drafted one budget, checked flights, and I had started backgrounding for the trip when I received an email from the doubting Chinese manager: "It's not possible to withdraw your passport. The Chinese embassy says they can't pull your passport and visa application without affecting the others in the packet for the trip you were initially supposed to go on."

Essentially, if my passport were removed, it would jeopardize other applications and passports with it.

My manager told me to stand down. Rather than pulling strings or calling in favors to make this happen, she felt it was a better strategy to put the group's need before the individual. With my Chinese management, motives were never clear. I began to wonder if my managers had decided they didn't want me to go after all, but chose to save face by letting the bureaucracy capture my passport.

My blood began to boil.

By this time, I had stayed in one place long enough to meet a great guy and start the adventure of settling down. This was something I had put off for years not knowing how to balance the type of work and life I sought with childbearing, much less child-rearing. My husband is a steady, calm match for my head-strong, high-risk, and sometimes fool-hardy passions. He has a particularly attractive strut in a cowboy hat and boots which made him the perfect yin to my yang. But his work meant travel for him, too, and that meant compromise.

I was six months pregnant with our second daughter, and I knew it was important to my professional momentum to make this trip now before going on maternity leave. Without my passport, I could not go on this state visit which was something I had been dreaming about all year. The deadline to turn in the papers was Saturday at noon, just two and a half days away! I was not going to let collectivism and group-think win the day.

I texted my core group of ladies, my coach, and my husband for prayer. Then I put my network to work (Lesson 8). I called a friend who is an executive at a big company, travels a lot, and has waged these prayer battles in the professional world before. She walked me through the details and we realized it came down to timeline. If I could get the passport back, I had a fighting chance. All the other paperwork was easy.

I prayed, "Lord, you know I want to go. If you want me to go, too, please open the doors. Please continue to give me peace about pursuing other ways of getting this passport back."

I spoke to my coach. He emailed: "The key is to stay in HIS peace. Keep asking Him what His plan is. If it's in HIS plan for you to go, no one can stop it. And vice versa."

I reached out to a political contact at the embassy and my trusty Asia affairs spokesperson at the National Security Council's office for advice. Both recommended getting the Chinese embassy press office involved to advocate for me. I followed up.

The next morning, I asked the work colleague who had filed my initial paperwork at the embassy how I could identify my passport and visa application for the embassy. She gave me two ticket numbers. My passport was identified with a visa application which was one of nine within those two ticket numbers. I would have to get someone to release my passport and visa application without affecting the other eight applications within the group.

I started calling people at the White House, at the United States State Department, the National Security Council, anyone who had any experience with Chinese visas or the embassy. By the end of the day, I had a contact at the embassy who thought she could help. We spoke, she told me what documents I needed, and how to use her name. She told me to call the next morning after she spoke to someone in the consular office about pulling my passport as a favor.

I welcomed friends from overseas that night and explained our day off the next day would be interwoven with other work duties. They were extremely generous and patient. I wanted to take them to the White House to tour around, but I also needed to attend a briefing I helped organize for foreign media reporters ahead of a major foreign policy announcement by the president.

Friday morning, I drove my two-year-old daughter, her au pair, and my two friends into the city praying for the best. I planned to attend

PICTURED: (Top) President Donald Trump takes questions from the press on the South Lawn of the White House. (Bottom) Me in Beijing outside the Forbidden City, 2017.

the briefing, send the notes to my colleagues, take my friends to the White House, and took on faith that somehow—if God willed it—my passport would be released.

Before the briefing, I called my new contact at the embassy and she had some news. The embassy would release the passport if I used her name at pickup.

I immediately called the doubting Chinese manager. I wanted to let her know I had a chance at getting the passport without endangering anyone else's application. But I also wanted her to know I did not want to pursue that option if I did not have her permission to do so. She sighed, said it was so complicated, but she thought I should try. This enabled me to show her respect as a leader and also allow her to make the decision. It was the culturally competent step to take in this situation.

As I was planning to entertain my friends, I passed all the information on to the colleague who had been helping with the original visa application and had already attempted getting my passport released. She speaks Mandarin and does this work for others in our company. I got an email back saying she was out of the office, but could her boss and a courier service take care of it? I followed up, asking her boss for contact information for the service. I was worried that without me staying involved this would not work out.

I went to tend to my friends. We walked to the White House gate. My daughter and I went through security, and I caught a whiff of a stinky diaper. I'd have to change this one in the press bathroom and hoped it wouldn't be too bad!

But I knew it would be and the briefing room bathrooms had no accommodation for diaper changing. I was fortunate to just have somewhere to pump breastmilk, quite frankly.

Neither of my friends were allowed through security because their information had not been green-lighted by the secret service.

Disappointed, I asked the press office to reapply for them while we went to lunch. I wanted to change that stinky diaper and get us all some food.

Changing that diaper was something the whole restaurant got to share in. My daughter, low on blood sugar, had a massive temper tantrum inside the echoey fast-food bathroom. She writhed on the floor, screamed, and tried to take her clean diaper off as soon as it was put on.

Her au pair helped me wrestle her back into her clothes, but my daughter then took the tantrum to the dining area, writhing around for what felt like hours. At almost six months pregnant, I wasn't really supposed to be lifting her—but I put her over my shoulder, took her outside, and tried to calm her down. I caught glimpses of colleagues in their suits as I walked by with a siren on my shoulder shouting, kicking, and screaming. We came back inside only for her to start up again until my friend took her in her arms and stroked her hair.

I was exhausted and it was only 11:30! We got through lunch, swung by the bank, and agreed my friends would go touring while the au pair, my daughter, and I would try to chase my visa. I tried to walk us back to the office before realizing six blocks could take 60 minutes. I called the White House travel office to get my account opened while holding my daughter's hand as she climbed a monument in Lafayette Park.

I talked to my boss to update him on the situation, asking him if he'd seen the people I needed around. He had, but "not recently." My daughter climbed on a dried-up fountain. She didn't want to walk. I didn't want to carry her. We grabbed a cab for those six blocks. I thought if my daughter could get a nap in the car and the au pair could rest, maybe I could run to the office and get some of this done myself.

Then I spoke to my doubting Chinese manager to update her. She said I could only go with a doctor's note allowing me to travel when that pregnant. I answered I would get that to her ASAP.

After hearing nothing for five hours, I arrived on the second floor of our office, miraculously to see the exact person I needed to speak to. He said he had not done anything about getting my passport from the embassy because he didn't have permission from the same doubting Chinese manager to make any decisions.

So, we called her together. I answered her questions about what type of costs the trip would incur and what type of access we would have. I said I would take care of the passport recovery effort on my own. I was finally given the address to go to, told how to recover the tickets tied to my passport and visa application, and how to use that ticket to get my passport and the other information I obtained from the embassy press contact.

"You better hurry," he added. "I think they close at 2:00." Looking at my phone, I realized it was 1:30.

Great, I thought, this whole thing is going to come down to not enough time, even if I have a will and a way!

I ordered an Uber. His GPS said I would arrive at 2:05. "God," I prayed, "I need a miracle. If You want me to go, I need to have enough time to get the tickets and the passport."

I called my boss, telling him I was on my way. If nothing else, I could say I'd done everything I could to get on that trip. He promised to draft the documents I needed from him as soon as I had the passport in hand. He was hedging his bets, too.

From the car, I called the travel company holding the tickets. I noticed the low phone battery and prayed for it to last as long as I needed. I spoke softly, calmly, politely, trying to hide the frantic feeling inside. I asked if they could pull the tickets now to save me time. I would pick them up and take them to the visa office one floor below. He agreed to do so. I asked him what time the consular office closes.

He said, "They close at 2:30."

"Wow, Lord! You gave me more time!" I prayed.

I got to the travel office at 2:15, praying for no line.

No line. I grabbed the tickets, ran to the elevators, pressed the floor button, and hurried into the consular office.

The security guard smiled. I told him what I was trying to do. "Everything has been so hard today," I said. "I need this to go right!"

"Everything at this office is hard," he said. "It's not your fault."

He gave me two pickup window numbers, took me through security, and showed me where to sit while I waited.

After being turned away from one window, I had to wait again for the right window. There, I explained the situation just as my embassy contact had instructed.

The gentleman smiled, said he would be happy to return my passport and withdraw my tourist visa application. He handed me a faded, over-copied form in Chinese and English to fill out. I quickly did so.

He went to get my passport.

When that passport was placed in my hand, I was overwhelmed with happiness and gratitude. Before leaving, I hugged the security guard at the door who had been so kind.

"I didn't know if this would happen," I explained, emotional.

On the way out, another man suggested I get a second passport so this couldn't happen to me again. Great idea!

I wrote to my coach: "Praise the Lord, I got my passport back!" I texted to my prayer chain: "I still must get a new visa, but this was the harder part! Thank you! GOD is working! I am crying."

"More miracles happening than you may be aware..." wrote back my coach.

I returned to the office and prepared my new visa application. My photographer colleague had prepared everything he needed just in case I could get my passport released.[1] I delivered the paperwork together later that day. We were the first reporters from a Chinese network to cover an American president's state visit to China inside the operations of the White House.[2]

---

1 https://www.youtube.com/watch?v=p2wagmitZcE
2 https://www.youtube.com/watch?v=zEjL0H3L9qU

▶ LESSON 13

Get a second passport! At the time of this writing, it's possible to get a second passport with a five-year time horizon by writing to the passport office and telling them you have a current one already in process at another embassy but need this one to travel. Provide the dates. Pay to expedite. It's a vital tool for high velocity travel. And don't be afraid to ask for help at every turn. You never know who in your network will have the answer you need—especially on days when everything seems hard.

Chapter 14

THE RUN-AROUND
IN SHANGHAI

Shanghai, China

November, 2018

A YEAR LATER, I was back in China. This time, I would be reporting and anchoring during the CIIE, China's first International Import Expo. It was to be held at a large facility just outside Shanghai. This was China's chance to show how many countries around the world wanted to export to its market of 1.5 billion people.

Back in the United States, trade war tensions were heightened, and the rhetoric was escalating to match. There was no interest in Washington, D.C. to send anyone of a high rank inside the U.S. government. This would only further underscore the contrast between countries siding with trade to China versus trading with the United States.

Thousands of journalists from China and around the world were converging on Shanghai to witness the turnout, the grand-opening speech of President Xi Jinping, and what large business deals would materialize. All of these would be scrutinized for the implications on global trade as well as the global economy.

My photographer colleague and I arrived in Shanghai by train from Beijing. We had wanted the experience of taking one of the high-speed trains in China, those we'd heard so much about. The experience was clean, fast, and efficient, though not a good match for storing the loads of heavy equipment we brought on the trip.

We were met in the train station by a doe-eyed young female employee from Beijing named Shao Yan. She was honored at the opportunity to participate in an important event for the network, one in which she took nationalistic pride. While her title was "producer" she met very few of the requirements one would meet in a Western newsroom to gain that title. We knew she was mostly there to report back on us to Chinese authorities. She was, to be honest, our "minder."

That alone made me all the more determined to use my influence and status as a Western journalist to help her understand what a producer did—to somehow lift the curtain on what an amazing lifestyle and profession searching for truth actually is. I wanted to help empower her to ask questions, advocate for herself, and seize this opportunity—not to simply check a box on the party playbook, escort American journalists, and keep them from uncovering or reporting anything less favorable to the party. I wanted to help her learn skills she could leverage to advance her own career.

She was an invaluable partner getting us where we needed to go. Mandarin is an incredibly difficult language to master and we needed help communicating everywhere we went. China's daily life is so integrated into technology, it's virtually impossible to navigate without a host of Chinese apps which allow you to search for, acquire, and pay for services through your phone which is connected to your national identity card and bank account (I had neither).

Imagine if you could not use Google Maps or GPS to get around, Uber or Lyft to hire for transportation, or a credit card to pay for it? All of these equivalent functions exist in China but only through Chinese technology interfaces. Most of their Western competitors are completely blocked or quickly copied and reproduced by a Chinese counterpart. You literally need a Chinese identity to function independently there.

One of the most important qualities in a fixer, or producer, is that they understand how to bend the rules. That's a rare find in any country, but particularly in China where bending the rules can get you thrown into jail. Young Chinese are educated to be devoutly patriotic. Since the 1989 Tiananmen Square massacre, when student protestors were slaughtered for demanding more democratic rights, Beijing wanted to avoid questions that led those students to stand up to their government. Ever since, young Chinese are taught that national pride in country and membership and loyalty to the Communist party, are inseparable. Under President Xi Jinping, the country has also further emphasized rejecting Western models of government in favor of the Chinese Communist Party's track record on providing its people with decades of stability and prosperity. Fewer and fewer Chinese believe the gunning down of those students was unwarranted, much less a crime.

I knew there would be moments of tension between what Shao Yan believed and what I knew to be the truth. At the same time, I underestimated how difficult it would be to mix her inexperience, reluctance to question authority, and obsession with following the rule of "causing no trouble" when entering the huge exposition center on the outskirts of Shanghai.

That first day, the network wanted us to do live shots from outside the venue and go back and forth inside the venue. They had no appreciation for the logistics and how difficult such a request would be. In addition, no one had done an advanced dry-run of how long transportation would take, distance between parking and entrance, the multiplicity of hurdles we would encounter, and how to navigate them. We arrived on

PICTURED: (Top) I pose with female taxi drivers in a fleet of Shanghai taxis. (Bottom) Me and producers pose while waiting in line to enter the CIIE convention space.

the media bus to take us to the venue with plenty of time to get there in advance, applying my lessons from Chapter 11.

When we arrived a half hour later, the landscape was a maze of barriers designed to funnel us into specific entrances for specific credentials. This was the first day of the expo, and security was extra tight because President Xi Jinping was due to speak and open the event.

The bus dropped us off in the parking lot, and we all walked through the lot into a series of cattle shoots to wait for the first credential check. After going through that, security pointed us toward a bridge between the parking lot and the building. As we began to climb the stairs to the bridge, we noticed the top of the staircase was blocked off. This was not a viable way in. We retraced our steps and found ourselves, for the next hour, going in circles. Every time Shao Yan asked for help from a security guard or police officer, she got a new set of directions. And yet we continued to blindly follow these directions which could not possibly have been accurate.

I continued to push Shao Yan to be less of a follower and more of a leader. "Ask the other journalists how are they getting in?" I offered. "Have longer conversations with the police officers. Make sure they understand you are getting conflicting information and just want to enter the darn building! Tell them who you are and who you work with and that they can help reflect well on their nation to a press corps of outsiders, rather than looking like a bunch of disorganized, compliant sheep."

But it was just not happening. And then I lost my cool. Filled with frustration, I burst out forcefully, yelling at a security guard when he tried to keep me from crossing an empty street to get to the next point where we could enter the facility. He screamed back. In that instant, I lost more than my cool. I lost the chance to influence this young woman.

I could see a look of terror cross Shao Yan's face at the thought that she would get in trouble for my behavior. And if that behavior was interpreted as disrespectful and arrogant, as opposed to brave and self-possessed, she would in turn be shamed. I had failed to fully grasp the impact of my actions. She underscored that saying, "We were specifically told we can't get in trouble with the authorities. We can't cause trouble."

I got defensive. "Of course, you were told that," I replied. "I don't want to get into trouble either, but that doesn't mean I can't question a security guard who is repeatedly giving us poor information."

I had a fleeting feeling of dread that I could be locked up for lesser things, so I had better tread lightly. At the same time, continuing in circles was untenable.

I reasoned with myself, and with her, that we would be failing in our mission if she didn't fight harder to make our deadline.

"Listen, people are depending on us to get to the right location and do a live cross," I said. "And they are spending thousands of dollars to make it happen. We can't let them down! It's your responsibility to make this happen. You've got to do something!"

Eventually, we found our way. But I maintain this was despite those security guards and Shao Yan's inability to critically think or convince the police our mission was vital.

It was not the only time her penchant for rule following would become a source of conflict. On another day, we chose to take a taxi to the location, rather than the press bus to enable us to better use our time to gather additional elements for our stories. As we entered the ring roads around the conference center, I saw fewer road blocks, but lots of barriers and police officers at the intersections directing traffic. Invariably they would wave us on before even ascertaining what we were trying to accomplish. They seemed to see their function as simply keeping us moving as opposed to helping us get inside.

Frequently, a photographer colleague would cajole our guide into acquiescing to what she must have thought were outrageous demands.

I needed to get to a position where a camera operator was already set up for live programming. I asked Shao Yan to see where we could disembark from the taxi. But this time, neither she or the taxi driver were interested in breaking any rules.

But I was determined to get out of the taxi at a point reasonable to walk and enter. I had already tested the back doors where I was sitting and they were set to lock. I quietly rolled down my window and grabbed a hold of the handle on the outside of the car. As we slowed for an intersection, I opened the door, thanked the driver, and jumped out.

"Come along!" I called to Shao Yan.

She followed, apologizing profusely in Chinese to the driver. When we caught up to each other, she looked at me with eyes full of anxiety mixed with anger. She explained the driver could lose his driving permits for not following police orders.

"He, and you, gave me no other option," I responded. "If you don't solve the problem, I will. We can't be late, and we can't miss our commitments because of security issues. This is what a field producer does."

It was a ham-handed attempt at some tough love, I admit. I regret I wasn't kinder and more understanding of her fears. At the same time, I felt there was value in shocking her just enough to show her that the world would not come crashing down if we questioned or challenged authority or a senseless rule. Even now, I continue to feel this is an important area for me to make an impact.

I remember fondly a Chinese colleague who embodied courage of conviction, but only up unto a point. She showed me it was possible in a Chinese and party-dominated context to question. Often, her independent streak and unwillingness to follow along made her a pariah among our Chinese colleagues but endeared her to the Western journalists in the office. We had many wonderful conversations about life, our kids, religion (a taboo subject for many Communist party members) and Western values. She and I were able to identify what we liked and didn't from the other person's culture and country. It was healthy, dynamic, informative.

I recall one particular conversation when she accompanied me to church to see what an American church service was like. I asked her about a particular tenant of Chinese political dogma and ran head-long into her red line. She was unwilling to budge on that point. I remember less the issue upon which we diverged than I do the fact she was intractable. But this, I could respect. She had engaged me with intellectual curiosity and seemed interested to truly understand.

Aside from the ways in which we differed, I found Shao Yan to be an excellent teacher about her generation and its comfort with big tech and Big Brother. She showed me how she could do almost everything she needed to do on her phone—ordering food, navigating the city, ordering a taxi, or paying for the subway.

At one point, we did a story at a Kentucky Fried Chicken in a Shanghai mall where you could pay with facial recognition. Later, I asked her if she was concerned the government had so much access to her personal information, even the balance in her bank account. She seemed entirely unperturbed. I described how much it bothered me to think my government could see the same information I considered private. The concept of privacy elicited another blank look. Shao Yan explained she felt safer with these technologies and was pleased her country had afforded her such advancements in lifestyle and quality of life. The tradeoff, it seemed, was worth it to her.

Shao Yan's general attitude towards technology, as well as how she could use it so effortlessly, was a big takeaway for me. In all candor, I hope we both exchanged some ideas the other had never encountered. That's a true win-win in the end.

▶ LESSON 14

Asking someone from a different culture to go beyond their cultural norms without preparation or notice is unrealistic and unkind. Chinese culture is uncomfortable with acting as an individual and adamantly against conflict with authority.

Here's a better approach. Set an expectation that conflicts will occur. To avoid bitterness or misunderstanding, agree from the outset that you are teammates engaged in achieving the same goal and that success will be determined through teamwork and creative problem solving.

Chapter 15

CONFLICT IN A CHINESE CONTEXT

Washington, D.C

September, 2018

WAS IN THE makeup room when my phone rang the alert. Wall Street Journal: DOJ (Department of Justice) requires Chinese state media to register as a foreign agent. I read the headline, heart in my throat. "This is my red line," I thought to myself.

The Foreign Agent Registration Act (FARA) is a United States law which imposes disclosure requirements and other legal obligations on any entity that becomes designated as a "foreign agent." FARA is a well-known regulation in the lobbying community, but up until then was rarely applied to media. The law was originally enacted in 1938 to prevent foreign propaganda in the run-up to World War II. It was meant to be a deterrent and was redeployed with additional frequency under the Trump administration to curb Russian and Chinese influence through media outlets like Sputnik and *CGTN America*.

During my time at *CGTN America*, I experienced an amount of journalistic independence comparable to my jobs in Western newsrooms. While the Trump administration may have assumed we were told what to write and report, that was not my experience. Any bias was more likely to be one of shining a narrow spotlight on issues important to Chinese interests—and hence ignoring stories the Western media would cover—as opposed to outright fabrication. Nonetheless, the pressure to tell more of the Chinese perspective to the exclusion of other perspectives did increase as time went on. That coupled with the FARA designation led to ethical concerns I increasingly struggled to reconcile. Ultimately, I could not.

"Will I have the courage to leave?" I asked myself in the moment. The first stage of shock and anger washed over me. I'm in the make-up chair trying to hold back the tears. The make-up artist offered me a tissue.

I have to calm down. It is going to be okay.

I'm about to anchor an hour-long program. I need to pull it together.

I'm not a lobbyist. I'm a journalist. I know that about myself.

I'm scared. I have two little girls at home.

On the one hand, I trust God will provide financially if I leave this job. But on the other, I want my girls to know that conviction takes courage. I don't want my children to grow up thinking beliefs don't come without sacrifice.

I asked my manager by text: "Have you asked your boss what this means?"

She responded an hour later with a denial: "It's not true. They haven't asked us to register."

But I knew it was only a matter of time. The relationship was heating up. I didn't want to be caught in the crossfire. I didn't want to be a casualty of the United States/China trade war.

My phone started buzzing with text messages from sources wondering if I've seen the report. I texted a reply with my conviction: "I'm still trying to learn what's going on. But I know that I'm a journalist, not a lobbyist."

PICTURED: (Top) Me on set. (Bottom) I took this photo as Liu He, top economic aid to Chinese President Xi Jining, conversed about trade priorities with President Donald Trump in the Oval Office, 2019.

Weeks later, I attended a happy hour with other White House correspondents and struck up a conversation with a National Security Council spokesperson. He asked me why I hadn't been around much, and I shared my concerns about the FARA designation. He seemed genuinely concerned about how this would impact me personally, and it was the first time I felt encouraged. I finally felt like somebody in my government cared.

Up until that point, I had been feeling persecuted by the Trump administration—not by the individuals I worked with and gleaned information from per se, but from the machine of forces buffeting the United States/China relationship which made me a target as the White House Correspondent for a Chinese network. Of course, the domestic press corps felt much the same way. That can happen when the U.S. president refers to the media as "the enemy of the people."

About a month later, I sat in the newsroom. We were listening to the vice president of the United States attack China and its state media, including our employer.

People were angry, reactive, sullen.

I was grateful another reporter on the White House beat was taking the lead on the story. I hadn't expected to feel as concerned, worried, and personally attacked as I did, but those feelings were real. My government was perfectly happy to allow me to be a casualty of the trade war to make a point, despite the reality that a Chinese company was providing good jobs and security for Americans.

I continued to pray for God's peace amid the storm. It seemed the radio station played just the right songs of comfort at just the right times, reminding me God's hand is bigger than my current circumstances.

My fellow coworkers seemed to acquire a dark humor, trying to make light of the situation. These were good journalists, decent and kind people, with a dark sense of humor.

"The American people deserve to know," Vice President Mike Pence intoned, that Beijing is employing "propaganda to advance its influence and benefit its interests in the United States. China is also applying this power in more proactive ways than ever before, to exert influence and interfere in the domestic policy and politics of our country."

I had never understood that to be our mission. Instead, like other employers seeking to exploit an imbalance in perspective, *CCTV America* and later *CGTN America* was the international arm of state television being used to tell China's story, to explain its perspective. As a journalist, I felt that was an important endeavor. I had come to learn how to balance stories against an inherent Western bias. This was an important function of what we did, particularly because China's role in the world was rising, and still it had yet to find a constructive voice publicly. There was little understanding of China's role in the world besides its impact on the global economy and trade. I felt it was a worthwhile goal to understand what makes China unique, even apart from the influence of the Communist Party, and communicate that to a world wondering how to interpret its advances in global institutions like the United Nations, the World Health Organization, and others.

We had gained a following of global viewers and policymakers in the United States. They sought out that balance, since more often than not, they perceived the heavy handprint of the Chinese Communist Party (CCP) on editorials and programming based in Beijing as opposed to the Americas, Europe, or Africa. Yet as a correspondent who had established journalistic credibility prior to my stint at *CGTN America*, I was grateful that while some in the Trump White House sought me out in scorn, most engaged professionally with me and my questions, including the president.

"Vice President Mike Pence says 70 million people are watching us. Why don't you give us a try?" someone quipped.

"We'll start a band called the FARAs..." said another, riffing on the Foreign Agent Registration Act under which we had reportedly been asked to register.

By the beginning of 2019, we learned the truth. *China Global Television Network* had in fact registered as a foreign agent, upon the United States Department of Justice's request. They did so without any transparency or regard for the implications for employees and their livelihoods. Under FARA, the Justice Department can demand contracts, benefits, and income statements for those who work at a FARA-designated company. The *CGTN America* brass did not disclose the registration prior to renegotiating employee contracts, and they only admitted it under intense questioning by employees at least six months after the initial public reports.

In all honesty, none of us were surprised that they had made the decision to register. It seemed it was done with the hope to tamp down the tensions which had begun to escalate between Washington, D.C. and Beijing. Once we too had reviewed the criteria for registration, we saw little wiggle room to avoid the same fate. Culturally, it made sense they had chosen to try and de-escalate through compromise. Furthermore, management wanted to keep operating at all costs. And because the FARA designation represented no penalty to the Chinese nationals, it was a safer play to keep the group happy than making decisions to appease the American group of employees.

China is still learning how to advocate for itself it the public fora. In many ways, Western employees contributed to its effort to learn. When we began in 2011, there were no regular briefings from the government ministries for the press. There were few, if any, press materials and English translations on ministry websites and rarely were there any opportunities for reporters to question public officials.

By the time I left *CGTN America* in early 2019, the Chinese public relations effort had morphed from defense to offense. Chinese diplomats and government officials had become emboldened on social media. They joined sites blocked in China such as Twitter, often leading the charge to push a response and counter narrative to any accusations made against them—whether it was allowing COVID-19 to spread intentionally, or undermining the national trade order by self-identifying as an emerging economy under World Trade Organization rules. They pushed alternate narratives to justify government and Communist Party actions without waiting for a criticism. The irony of the vice president's speech in 2018 is that *CGTN America* was then far less a vehicle for propaganda than it would become.

▶ LESSON 15

There's no expectation of transparency about conflict in a Chinese context, so there is none. Had I invested time earlier in relationship-building with my Chinese managers and joined regular lunches, exchanges on mutual interests, or outings with my Chinese colleagues, I might have had a better chance of navigating that opaqueness. While I can't know for certain, understand that building a rapport with your colleagues can serve to cushion the inevitable miscommunication you'll face in any workplace, especially one with a diverse culture.

Chapter 16

THE AMERICAN "BRAND" IN VIETNAM

Hanoi, Vietnam

February 2019

IN FEBRUARY OF 2019, I got my last assignment at *CGTN America*: "We'd like you to go to Hanoi, Vietnam, to cover the next round of talks between North Korean leader, Kim Jong Un and United States President Donald Trump."

What a great opportunity! Not only would I be back on the trail following a fascinating and polarizing president, but I would finally visit the country my brother had called home for almost two years.

The photographer and I decided to take a flight through Tokyo so we could also spend some time there on the return trip. I slept as much as I could on the flight to Tokyo. I knew there would be little sleep over the next 10 days as I did live programming for bureaus in two time zones.

We touched down in Hanoi. Even though it was February, it was in the 60s, damp, and rainy. Hanoi is located just 1,455 miles north of the equator. Much warmer than what we left behind in Washington, D.C.

Like many Americans, for me Vietnam is a word which evokes feelings of a war the United States didn't win. It's an incredibly painful and controversial part of American history. What I discovered on my first visit to Vietnam, was that there is a long history of conflict and reconciliation there. It's been said we don't know the value of peace until we've been at war. Perhaps that's why Hanoi has so many reminders of conflict.

At the Vietnam Museum of the Revolution, you can see the totality of generations of war on the Vietnamese people. The outdoor exhibits alone take you back to 1954 when a nine-year resistance culminated in the battle of Dien Bien Phu when the French colonialists lost to the Vietnamese. The destroyed carcasses of B-52 bombers shot down during the "Vietnam War" or, as it's known there, the "United States sabotage war of North Vietnam" dot the campus.

There are torpedoes from the former Soviet Union co-opted by the Vietnamese communists to drive away the United States forces during that war. American tanks, a Chinook helicopter, jets, and B-52 bombers complete the collection.

I visited one neighborhood where a pond still houses a piece of a fallen B-52 bomber. It has become like a sculpture in that context, but to my eyes was still a jarring reminder.

The Vietnamese fought the Chinese in a protracted and violent border war from 1979 to 1990. Today, they are still sparring over rights to islands in the South China Sea. But at the same time, they cooperate in a variety of ways economically. China was the second largest investor as a country in Vietnam in 2019.

And yet, there was little to no mention of that history at the Hoa Lo Prison, also known as the Hanoi Hilton. This museum focuses more on the conflicts with the French and Americans. I expected to see more information on display concerning the American POW's here. Nope. Just two rooms emphasizing the "resort-like conditions" they were housed in, complete with volleyball courts and their glorious release.

PICTURED:
(Top-L) French guillotine in the Hoa Lo Prison. (Top-R) Warplane at the Vietnam Museum of the Revolution. (Bottom) Le Dang Doanh, former Vietnamese economic advisor during the Doi-Moi reforms speaks with me.

"Was this a hotel or a prison?" I thought to myself.

United States Senator and former United States presidential candidate, John McCain, spent five and a half years in this prison. He was held in such a way he never regained the ability to lift his arms above his head. Rather than a photograph of his torture, there's a black and white image of him receiving medical treatment.

But if the Vietnamese were known as terrible tormentors during the conflict in the 1960s and 70s, they also knew what it was to be victims of cruelty and brutal treatment by the French colonialists. The museum showed the small cells where famous revolutionary Vietnamese communists suffered and where groups of men, women, and children were shackled side-by-side in large groups seated on hard wooden tables.

The most impactful thing for me was where a guillotine towered over the room. A sign told the frequency with which it was used to terminate prisoners.

Today, Vietnam has relationships with all its former enemies—France, China, and the United States. People from these countries are welcomed visitors and entrepreneurs. You'll see the influences of all those countries in the city's architecture, the faces of the people, and the types of businesses flourishing there.

When I queried people about this ability to forgive and move on which seems engrained in the culture, locals pointed to the impact of Confucianism on the Vietnamese. The teachings of Confucius hold a premium on restoring harmony. It's a remarkable attribute to witness in a population that has experienced repeated horrors through years of war.

It makes me wonder if the West prioritized balance and harmony, rather than "winning," would we see progress in areas where we've not yet achieved peace and unity?

During my stay, I was able to spend time with two men who lived through the Vietnam war on opposite sides. Chuck Searcy was an American GI, and Nguyen Qui Duc was a local boy whose father—a

South Vietnamese civil servant—was taken by the North Vietnamese as a political prisoner. I wanted to understand their experience with the conflict and the harmony first-hand.[1]

"The amazing thing was that we were welcomed by everyone with open arms," said Chuck Searcy, who returned to Hanoi in 1992. Searcy now lives in Hanoi permanently and works with a nonprofit on reversing the damage of the defoliant, Agent Orange, and landmines which are still killing and maiming the innocent decades after the war ended.

"I felt a great responsibility and a great opportunity to represent the sentiments of a lot my friends," he said. "I think [my friends] would very much support the effort to rebuild the relationship between the United States and Vietnam and recognize we should never have been enemies."

Nguyen Qui Duc, now an entrepreneur who runs a local pub, lost 16 years with his dad during the war. His father was held at the infamous Hanoi Hilton before being shipped to a re-education camp.

"People say, 'how can you forgive the fact that your father was taken away and you lived 16 years without your father?'" he told me. "I say, 'well, if I'm bitter about it, it's not going to get me anywhere. It's not going to get me the 16 years back.'"

He believes Vietnam made the right decision after the war with the United States ended. Vietnam needed friendship with the West and the economic incentives which come with it to rebuild. "If you compare the 20 years of conflict with the benefit of being friends with the world, then the choice is clear," Duc said. "You make friends."

Much of the country has benefitted from a closer economic relationship with the West and an openness to capitalism, or as the Vietnamese call it, a "socialist-oriented market economy."

Le Dang Doanh, a former Vietnamese government economist during the "Doi-Moi" economic reforms told me, "[There's] no way to integrate with the world economy without normalizing relations with Washington, D.C. [The government] must give their power up to the

1 https://www.youtube.com/watch?v=3YkGvANVun4

business, private sector, to the market, and they need to learn how to keep the market well-developed in a balanced way, and it is not easy."

Nearly 40 years on, the economic experiment is bearing fruit. There is an energy and a dynamism of a fast-growing economy which at times has matched the six to seven percent growth rate of China. The diplomatic benefits have altered the view of America for a whole new generation of Vietnamese and offered a brand-new vision of Vietnam to a whole new generation of Americans. President Bill Clinton famously said in his Hanoi speech in November, 2000, that for Americans, Vietnam would no longer be a war but a country.

These days, you will see faces from all over the world on the streets of Hanoi. That, too, is certainly hopeful. It shows reconciliation can happen, its benefits can form bonds that better both cultures, and that owning the truth of the past can pave the way for a promising future. It's a remarkable feat for the Vietnamese, one the cultures of the Middle East could certainly benefit from as well.

My father often tells a story about an Egyptian Coptic nun. My mother initially met her on an exchange of teachers at her small, private Mennonite school in rural Pennsylvania. This woman had grown up her entire life believing Egypt, not Israel, had won the 1967 war, also known as the Six Day War. I'm not sure how she explained why Israel never returned the Gaza Strip to Egypt or how those same people became the epicenter for the Arab-Israeli conflict we still see today. But her history which she firmly believed was not questioned until she ran across another culture which had a different history. By seeing Israel in light of this truth, and not in the history she had come to accept, you have to wonder if it could change the relationship between her and an Israeli. And could that change spread and form a partnership to find progress for a region?

This is why history is so critical to our perception—why it's important to know your own, but also to be willing to question your version of it.

▶ LESSON 16

Be aware your that ideas about other countries are frequently based in an Americanized version of their history. Likewise, their opinion of you may initially be based on their experience and education of your history. Be willing to question your version as you question that belonging to someone else.

Chapter 17

A WOMAN'S TOUCH IN HANOI

Hanoi, Vietnam
February 2019

THERE'S A STRIKING DIFFERENCE between the streets of Vietnam and China and those of the United States. In Hanoi, the faces on the street riding a multitude of mopeds are young and vibrant. The median age there is 30 years old.

There are dozens of cranes across the skyline and construction sites abound. On the way to our hotel, we drove on a road built just three years prior. You'd be hard-pressed to find a road that new in Washington, D.C.!

Old and new coexist. You'll see farmers working in the rice paddies, wearing cone-shaped, palm-leaf hats known as the "non." But you'll also pass factories producing concrete and see skyscrapers in the distance. There are also dozens of large office parks producing the latest technology in cell phones, television sets, other electronics, as well as NIKE shoes and other brand-named clothing.

In nearly 40 years since Vietnam's government began implementing its reforms, this country has been transformed. The young push for economic progress. They want what America has given its citizens, and the Communist party there is less heavy-handed. For example, the Chinese app, WeChat, which is heavily monitored in Beijing, is not the sole means of communication and electronic payment in Vietnam. In China, all other means are blocked without a personal VPN.

Residents in Vietnam, by contrast, prefer Facebook's WhatsApp. There's also fewer restrictions for foreign workers there. My brother operated as a digital nomad there for two and a half years, coming in and out on short-term visas. He worked as a freelance computer programmer with far lower overhead costs than if he had worked from the United States. That would be more complicated, if not impossible, to do in China.

In Hanoi, I very much appreciated the perspective and viewpoint of our fixer, Ha Ninh.

This lady is a smart mom of two who had married a Dutch executive. She was far more educated than required for the job she took with us. It was a treat to learn about Vietnam through her eyes.

In Lesson 10, I cautioned about over-relying exclusively on the narrative of permanent aid workers you meet in foreign places. I would say the same about translators/fixers. But I will also say I find it important to learn about countries and cultures from women and moms who often observe life, culture, and economy on more than just an intellectual plane. At times, these women are closer to issues of social and relational differences than men. I rely on them to add more color and texture to my understanding of new places and people.

One day, Ha and I took a "cyclo" tour in downtown Hanoi. I videoed her observations as we passed by the changes which had taken place visually, structurally, and historically since she was a young girl.[1]

"A lot of the Americans look at Vietnam as where they lost a war, the place where the communists ran the North," I observed. "But you've

1 https://www.facebook.com/cgtnamerica/videos/262815967937798

told me this city saw many more conflicts than just what we know as the Vietnam War."

She responded, "You know we had many conflicts with the French and had a hard time. In the American time, we had a lot of bombing."

We passed by rows of designer shops with flashy titles like Cartier and Prada, all within French architecture. We passed the French-designed opera house and various prominent hotels.

Ha has spent the past 10 years in Hanoi. She told me the city has become more expensive and full of high-rise buildings as thousands of people move there for better jobs and medical services. Ha has memories of not being able to find candy to purchase when she was a very little girl. Now, there are chocolate shops on the street corners along with French pastry bakeries.

We spoke about our children, their educations, hopes, and dreams. It broadened my understanding of what life is like in Vietnam and gave me a richer understanding of the culture.

Ha introduced me to Trang Tuyet Nga,[2] founder of the medical device manufacturer, MTTS. Nga was so moved by babies who died of breathing difficulties or jaundice complications that in 2003, she founded a medical device company. "I realized that with this very simple medical equipment, we can reduce the mortality rate and save more babies," she said.

Initially the company repaired imported machines, but now they manufacture them. In the years she's run her company, Nga has seen financial incentives tied to Vietnam's status as a developing economy disappear due to progress. When we spoke in 2019, she planned to move her operations into one of the city's large industrial parks which frequently come with economic incentives.

"We were the first company in Vietnam to make medical equipment, so that's why the government gave us a lot of privilege," Nga explained.

---

2 https://www.youtube.com/watch?v=_Y_0-IsKJ-s

PICTURED: Ha Ninh and I in between live shots at the Kim-Trump Summit in Hanoi, Vietnam.

The seed for the company began from the compassion and empathy a woman and mother feels for helpless babies. That's not to say a man doesn't feel the same things, but I'm not sure a man would have experienced the situation as she did. There is truly a connection women and mothers have, both to each other and to children, that I've only really noticed since I became a wife and mother myself.

This, too, is cultural distinction. It's worth being aware of how those differences change what we see and how we experience places and people—not only through their food and language, but through the way they interact with and treat genders.

When I first started working at *CCTV America*, I was the only female correspondent. When I left, it was actually the same. I was a single woman when I joined. I married my husband the second year I worked there. I had three female bosses, two of whom had children. I thought perhaps because of that, they would understand me on some level even if it wasn't a cultural one. There were, indeed, areas of commonality, especially once I began having children. But as a single woman, I struggled to connect with my female Chinese colleagues and my Chinese bosses.

Being a blonde-haired, Western woman working for Chinese television drew the attention of a slew of Japanese broadcasters. For a season, I was profiled on nearly every one of them as the American woman working for China. This gave my Chinese bosses the idea that they, too, should feature me in a profile showcasing their diversity.

The woman they asked to conduct the profile interview, Esther, and I had already established very different approaches to being reporters and women. In my experience, being strong, confidant, plain-spoken, asserting my turf, and approaching male colleagues as equals (or sometimes less than if they were more junior) were to my advantage in the rough-and-tumble world of political journalism. I wore that persona as a badge of honor. It was the opposite of how Esther approached interacting with men in our bureau.

She often called me "aggressive" in the interview as she fashioned her questions around what I thought made me successful in Washington D.C.'s journalism field. I repeatedly told her this term indicated something negative, and the better descriptor was "assertive," meaning I could hold my own. The finished product used the adjective "aggressive." I never really escaped that perception, constantly having to defend my reputation for being assertive, blunt, and direct. I don't apologize for it, but I sure had to defend and explain it over my tenure there.

Culturally, this assertiveness was not expected or respected in Chinese women. Esther giggled around my male colleagues even though she earned her MBA from Cambridge University. She would bat her eyelashes, ask the men simple questions, and coo at their answers. In time, I came to realize that this is part of what it still means to be a woman in Chinese circles. Being openly "strong" is not seen as an advantage. Those characteristics were never openly displayed by my female Chinese bosses, but reserved for conversations behind closed doors. Furthermore, a Chinese female colleague who did possess that level of confidence and directness in communication frequently got criticized and sidelined the same way I did. As I noticed cultural shifts within my newsroom, I also noticed them in myself.

Fast-forward to 2019. Seeking out moms has become a new lens for me to see the world. We all are looking for meaning and balance in our professions, for better futures for our children, and quality time with our significant others. There are layers of similarity as well as layers of difference. It's helpful to build on those commonalities when trying to form ties and contacts. For me, it's also a way to guard against my own biases.

Being a woman, a wife, and a mom is a common experience across cultures, even though so many things are different from country to country. Often, what we women commonly care about serves to ground me no matter what culture I'm in.

▶ LESSON 17

Culture is experienced differently by gender, and distinctly through our season in life. While it might seem obvious, it can still sneak up on you. My perspectives have changed from being a single woman, to becoming a wife, to bearing and raising children. There is a cultural richness to these seasons and the way gender interplays with them. It's important to learn about a culture and those who are a part of it through these attributes. I often wish I had done this more.

Chapter 18

THE MAN AT THE AIRPORT LOUNGE

Chicago Airport

March 2019

WHEN I WORKED AT *CGTN America*, one of the best parts of international travel was time spent in the luxuries of airport lounges. It's a privilege you only get if you're flying business or first class. On my last flight from Hanoi, I was in the Chicago airport lounge waiting to fly to Washington, D.C.

Jetlagged from the 16-hour flight from Tokyo to Chicago, I was ready to charge my devices and get some free food. I approached a middle-aged man, neatly dressed, who had a congenial expression and asked if he could watch my stuff while I got something to eat and drink. He kindly said yes.

I loaded up my plate on fruits and vegetables I wouldn't be seeing again on the flight home and got another cup of juice and coffee.

When I returned, we exchanged pleasantries. It came up that I was returning from Asia. He mentioned he'd done business there for years in banking. The conversation moved to the fact he wanted to write a book about a concept he found lacking in Eastern culture: absolute truth, which is indeed absolute.

"The concept of absolute truth is founded in Judeo-Christian, Greco-Roman thought," he explained, counting off those qualifiers on his fingers.

Suddenly, so many experiences from the past seven years of working for a Chinese company, struggling to understand the opacity, the decision-making, and the changing narratives around issues—like who owns islands in the South China Sea, what's the true nature of the Xinjiang Muslim work camps, and what really happened during the cultural revolution—all came into focus.

"You just put a frame on the last eight years of my life," I said. I never understood why these things didn't make sense to me. As a person of Christian faith, I believe there is one God, one path to Him, and one truth. While we may approach truth and describe it somewhat differently, it doesn't change. It has stayed the same since God created the heavens and the earth.

As a journalist, I believe absolute truth is there to discover, and it's my calling to uncover it. That doesn't mean all my sources, or even I, have the entire picture all the time. In fact, we almost never do. It just means it's our goal to find it.

But in a culture where the emperor decides what truth is, there is no absolute and independent truth. There is only a belief to justify, a decision to explain, and thus a fungible concept of fact that isn't immutable.

While the man in the airport lounge conceived of this paradigm as being East vs. West, I would argue, it's also authoritarian vs. democratic. You'll find that controlling truth is job number one for autocrats—whether its Russia's Vladimir Putin, Zimbabwe's Robert Mugabe, China's Xi Jinping, or Egypt's Abdel Fattah Al-Sisi.

It's imperative that you have this lens as you travel the world, or even move about your workplace, school, or community. People who have been raised in a culture or a country where the truth is fluid will bring that understanding of truth wherever they go. And it applies not only to history as we've previously discussed in Chapter 16, but how we define other ideas like rule of law or national identity. It's also something we must protect against as our history increasingly becomes written on the Internet, where content can be revised without notice, explanation, or justification.

Guard against the voices that say you can have your own truth. We all need to be thinking critically. This is not just the job of researchers or journalists. It's everyone's job. If you don't, you risk buying into a narrative not based in reality.

▶ LESSON 18

Concepts like justice, law, and truth are not defined
the same across various cultures. Understanding
the difference will help you communicate
about issues of fairness and right and wrong.
Understanding this notion is compatible with
the belief that truth exists and is discoverable.
You can be culturally appropriate about how you
discuss inconvenient truths. Sometimes a culture's
survival is built on having a clear definition of
these values. Other times, it's built on having an
intentionally vague notion of these concepts.

Chapter 19

UNITED NATIONS OR WHITE HOUSE FOREIGN PRESS GROUP?

Washington, D.C.

2012–2019

THROUGHOUT MY TENURE AS a White House Correspondent for *CCTV America*, and later for *CGTN America*, I had opportunities to employ my cross-cultural competency. I picked up new observations about interacting across multiple ethnicities and worldviews through my involvement with a group of foreign journalists covering the White House—called the White House Foreign Press Group or the WHFPG.

The group was the brainchild of Laura Haim, formerly the United States reporter for Canal Plus, one of the major television networks in France. We were a group of journalists from all over the world—India, Turkey, Morocco, Saudi Arabia, China, Taiwan, France, Germany, Luxembourg, Canada, Brazil, and a sizable media delegation from Japan. Our group did not include the BBC, Reuters, or Al-Jazeera as they were large enough to have their own individual briefing room seats and dedicated reporters on the White House beat.

Over the seven years of my involvement, we successfully made the case to the broader White House Correspondents' Association that foreign media could add value to our collective coverage. It would bring additional international context and language to foreign visits and global meetings such as the United Nations General Assembly, the G7, the G20 and the World Economic forum at Davos, Switzerland. For example, we routinely approached the embassy of the foreign leader ahead of visits for their goals, agenda, and the context around any ongoing negotiations underway between the United States and them. In return for our services, we received guaranteed access for one foreign "pool" reporter in each event where there were international guests.

Under the Trump administration, we greatly expanded the definition of international impact as so many of the policies pursued by that administration had international import. We also grew exponentially during those years as every country in the world sent additional reporters to Washington, D.C. to cover this polarizing American president.[1]

In addition to access, we secured real estate for our group. We shared a seat in the briefing room and a workspace, complete with a patch of Formica laminate and a broken office chair. But no one complained as any spot to sit and work was highly valuable. The entire area designated for our collective workspace was constructed in 1969 and 1970. It spans the swimming pool built for President Franklin Delano Roosevelt in 1933 and an additional two floors of work and broadcasting areas positioned between the West Wing and the White House residence. The now-drained swimming pool houses all the servers and electronics for the broadcast and radio networks as well as our connectivity to the Internet.

We took turns using our coveted assigned seat in the briefing room to ask a variety of foreign policy and monetary policy questions. Over

1 https://www.facebook.com/cgtnamerica/videos/1511124918982775

time, we became convinced we must use our workspace or it would be overrun by other media or photographers who were always looking for a place to rest their heads, bums, or gear while on-call.

As we grew in size and influence, I observed a keen difference between my foreign press colleagues and my fellow American journalists. International journalists appeared to revere the White House as the center of global power and influence. They cherished getting an opportunity to cover the leader of the countries they hailed from as they met with the United States president in the Oval Office. They seemed to have a great sense of place and history when they covered events inside the White House grounds.

I found some to be overly reverent as though they were in the halls of a king rather than an elected official accountable to the people. There were many who took their cues from the press handlers we called "wranglers." My foreign journalist colleagues frequently held back and missed opportunities to drop in at an office of a communications staffer as a result.

By comparison, my American colleagues often valued the privilege of covering the White House but took it more in stride. They were more assertive and even aggressive, particularly during the Trump administration. The longer I covered the presidency, the more I realized the American journalists actually knew more about the traditions and procedures for covering the White House than any incoming president did. They were the keepers of these traditions and provided some consistency across administrations.

I realized I needed to follow their lead in this respect. I needed to not accept where the president and his staff drew the lines, but rather where the White House Foreign Press Group had fought to have eyes—whether that was the president taking his wife out to a date (what if he gets assassinated and there's no press there to record his dying moments?) or riding on his plane on a foreign trip.

The White House Foreign Press Group varied greatly within its ranks across cultures. I perceived the Japanese and Chinese journalists to be fairly passive and deferential, often riding the coat tails of the more outspoken and assertive European and Middle Eastern reporters. Always playing mediator was our French-Canadian colleague, Richard Latendresse (Richard pronounced REE-shard). He always looked for the middle ground among our group. He avoided conflict, volunteered to take notes, and do the technocratic work that would keep him valuable to the group but not a threat to those who wanted title or position more than influence. Brilliantly played, *mon ami*! He is truly the Switzerland of the White House Foreign Press Group.

Cultural differences came out in the way we interacted with the White House staff, but also in the way we asked questions. In the briefing room, few of us were willing or prepared to verbally spar with a press secretary. When it came to sessions with ambassadors, we still asked questions with a respect and deference more indicative of diplomatic conversation than of the American tradition of an adversarial press corps.

I distinctly recall a meeting with the Belgian ambassador after the ISIS attacks in Paris in 2015. My colleagues asked plenty of great questions which helped us all better understand the situation. But they didn't question the law enforcement process, especially the law against police raids between 9:00 p.m. and 5:00 a.m. of private homes. In the United States, there's no curfew for the cops, no time in which your home can't be searched for evidence or seized if there's probable cause a crime is or has been committed there. I asked about whether Belgium was considering striking down the ban as a way of giving police a stronger tool in the fight against radicalized Islamic teenagers joining ISIS and other Jihad groups. The ambassador's answer made it clear the right to privacy inside someone's home superseded the rights of the police to find the perpetrators of such a heinous act. In a post 9/11 world, I found that perspective shockingly naive.

Oddly enough, the Japanese and Chinese journalists were somewhat friendly to each other. Their cultures typically have deep-seated hatred and mistrust of each other, so this was a refreshing exception. I thoroughly enjoyed working with my dear Chinese reporting colleague, Ching-yi Chang, initially of Phoenix TV and later of Shanghai Media. He was a ready decoder ring for my own colleagues and work environment and often helped me understand various idiosyncrasies of Chinese culture.

Our Japanese colleagues initially thought I was a sensation. They each asked me for interviews so they could profile me for their audiences. The blonde girl who works for Chinese television was quite an oddity to them. It didn't seem to matter that other Japanese television networks had already interviewed me. They all wanted to do what they had seen the others do. The Japanese were also quite proud nationalists. They had their own system of sharing resources, information and clips, and they never wanted to pass up any type of exclusive information—particularly on North Korea.

During the administration of President Obama, there was little engagement with the WHFPG in terms of offering tailored explanations for policy decisions to an international audience. We rarely had any run-ins, but our membership did not experience what I would consider to be active engagement either. For example, we never received a sit-down meeting with the press secretary at the beginning of the administration. Not until we had Josh Earnest, President Obama's last press secretary, did that occur. Earnest was a friend to the foreign media. He took the time to call on us by name. Since about 15 people were rotating the same seat and he had to know the rest of the briefing room's three or four dozen seats, this was a kind gesture that did not go unnoticed or unappreciated.

Like so many ironies during the Trump administration, we actually discovered a lot more engagement with a White House who wanted to be "America First." They had so little experience in government, and so much distrust of the domestic media who had covered them on the campaign, it played to our advantage to be foreign reporters.

As a reporter for a Chinese network, I found the door wide open to engage with the White House national security staff and the communications staff. They willingly arranged foreign press briefings around their trade agenda and international trips. We met with President Trump's Middle East Peace Advisor and son-in-law, Jared Kushner, ahead of the president's trip to Saudi Arabia in May, 2017. I later worked to book briefings with the Japanese, Korean, and Chinese embassies ahead of President Trump's first trip to Asia in November 2017. We similarly arranged background briefings for trips to Europe and the United Nations General Assembly.

The president had made a big show of pledging to be tough on China while on the campaign trail. I had initially feared I'd be boxed out of all press events to which I had a right to cover as a credentialed journalist at the White House. But this was not the case. The communications staff actually took an interest in reaching out to me. Over time, they made sure I was in the room for every major occasion in United States and China relations until I left the position.

Being a member of the White House Foreign Press Group required one level of cultural competence but taking on a leadership position in it necessitated a higher level.

Whether it was navigating the nationalistic tendencies of my Japanese media colleagues (who felt they should have a larger role due to their numbers but tended to rely on the group to provide information instead of digging for it themselves); or creating opportunities for our Brazilian reporter to hold and plan social events (which was part of how she met and retained sources culturally); or conversations and briefings around the Jewish-Palestinian issue which divided our group, I slowly assembled a cocktail of American individuality coupled with cultural understanding.

My American side relied on merit, hard work, and personal relationships to supersede the culture and reputation of my media outlet which was the subject of much skepticism in both White Houses I covered. By contrast, for many of my international colleagues, their identity was closely aligned to how important and revered their outlet was in their home country. Being treated as just another foreign reporter wasn't easy for those who worked for the likes of Le Monde or Al-Arabiya.

The most interesting exercise in bridging our cultural differences to achieve an outcome was when we made collective decisions as a group. At no time did I see how my colleagues understood our American democracy as clearly as when we met to vote on new officers of the group. They wanted to discuss everything completely, vote on every issue, and often argued over who could vote in certain instances.

The Japanese media delegation was a conundrum for the group. Had each of them been allowed to vote, they would have completely dictated the direction of the group, simply by their numbers. So we had them rotate their vote between four representatives.

We either renewed our officers or voted in new ones every six months. We used a conference room at the Associated Press building in Washington, D.C. for our meetings. We would pile in between other assignments to raise our problems and gather solutions. These problems were unique to foreign reporters unfamiliar with the ins and outs of the United States government and the behind-the-scenes workings at the White House. We could get lost in endless discussion and debate until someone on a deadline prompted us to vote or table the issue for a future meeting. It was rare to cut off a reporter in the interests of expediency, lest an allegation of being unfair or undemocratic be leveled.

My role as an officer of the White House Foreign Press Group began when Laura Haim, who would later receive the illustrious *Légion d'honneur* award in France for her journalism career, asked me if I could substitute for her at her job doing live shots in French for Canal Plus. I demurred, reasoning I already had a full time job and my French was not as *au courant* as I would have liked.

She later invited me to lunch at the Sofitel in downtown Washington, D.C. where we visited in French interjected with English when my vocabulary failed me. She recruited me to be a vice president, hoping to get me more involved so I could use my strong voice and credible presence at the White House on the group's behalf. Lalit Jha, the White House correspondent for the Press Trust of India (India's main wire service), ran for the office of president.

I agreed to run for vice president and within weeks we held our annual meeting to vote on the officers of the White House Foreign Press Group. This time, Lalit and I sailed through. Members were glad to have fresh blood with me and a steady presence in him.

Lalit was not the type of journalist or president to try to make news, hog the spotlight, or even advocate noisily for the group. He was, rather, the type to ask a very thoughtful, cerebral, and India-focused question at briefings. Lalit treated everyone with respect and deference. In the shark tank they call the White House press corps, that could be interpreted as timid and a doormat. And yet, on policy, he was dogged. I often found out in calls of my own that he was well-known to press liaisons for the National Security Council at the White House. But he did not seek to be close to the domestic press apparatus. This was a mistake a lot of the foreign journalists made. Relationships with the press secretary and his or her staff was ultimately the path to the inner circle, even if it was difficult territory to gain entry to as a foreign reporter.

I made a good sidekick for Lalit and tried to help my colleagues navigate the cultural barriers of a foreign (to them) government. We aimed to push our agenda which included more invites to White House off-the-record briefings, arrange our own information sessions at embassies, and in general increase access and information between the White House and the White House Foreign Press Group. I relied heavily on the First Amendment which I argued enshrined access for all journalists—even those from foreign outlets—to the administration, not just domestic outlets.

———————— ▶▶ ————————

Then one day, I decided to run for president of the White House Foreign Press Group. I had been asked to do so a few times by the stronger leaders. No reporter from an Asian outlet had ever held the position before so the Japanese press also supported my candidacy. At least, I thought that was the case.

On the day of the vote, there was a lengthy and loud debate as to whether a journalist from a state-run television network would be a help or a hindrance to the group. There was a deep divide among the journalists. Those who worked for private channels told us they could be more independent than those who worked for public or government channels. Often, a whisper campaign of "they're state-run" was enough to do-in anyone's candidacy from those positions, depending on their standing and respect in the broader press corps. Wherever there were journalists covering the White House for countries governed by authoritarian leaders or monarchs, there was a natural tension. But our group never had any regulations or bylaws against members of state-run media participating. Evidently, that too, was viewed as non-democratic.

I made the case I had editorial independence from Beijing, and at the time, I did. I always vowed I would leave if and when the mission to deliver news with a Chinese perspective turned into propaganda. I'm proud to say I did just that. Nonetheless, as an American journalist, I fully appreciated their concerns and certainly did not want my candidacy to do anything but help the group.

My colleagues saw my value and voted me in. I set about trying to prove I could do the job fairly, no matter who I worked for. I remained just six months in the position as the United States/China relationship increasingly proved fraught and would have been a disservice to the group had I remained in the position.

All things considered, those six months I served as president and the years preceding it where I became a larger voice in the organization provided some of the most varied and unique insights into cross-cultural competence I ever experienced. In truth, had I not already been a part of the WHFPG, I could never have attempted to navigate the melting pot of my *CGTN America* newsroom. At the same time, these journalists from around the world held up a mirror to the government we all covered. And what I learned through their eyes could not have been gleaned any other way.

▶ LESSON 19

In the White House Foreign Press Group,
we overcame our own internal cultural differences to
rally around an ideal sense of democracy and inclusion
to accomplish the goal of better covering the leader of
the free world. In many ways, what we established was
the best of all of us, working together to accomplish
an idea, not a tradition. But you'll find in order to
accomplish that synergy with a group of very diverse
people, you need a very clear, strong, and dominant
goal which everyone supports with the same intensity.

Chapter 20

YOU DON'T HAVE TO LOSE YOUR IDENTITY TO IDENTIFY WITH OTHERS

Everywhere

All the Time

THE LONGER I LIVE, the more connected the world gets. With any luck, the same will be true for you. When I started my career in journalism, newsrooms were not as diverse as they are now. The workplace of the future is likely to be mobile, international, and diverse culturally. A 2019 Institute for the Future study named cross-cultural competency one of the 10 most important skills for the workplace of the future.

My children are already growing up with a greater awareness of the world than I had in childhood. They'll have passports and language skills well before I did. Their workplaces will be far more likely to be a cornucopia of talent, ambition, and culture. You may have a Chinese-born manager, a European coworker, and an African client footing the bill for the project you're on. That requires you to know something about how to adapt your communication, your sense of time, and your understanding of truth to each individual's norms.

Cultural competency is not the idea that you are the same or have to believe the same things about life and death, truth, or justice as those you interact with. It's the idea that every person has intrinsic value and every person's perspective is important to understand so you can accomplish greater things together than apart.

If you have strong personal passions, moral convictions or religious beliefs, these shouldn't keep you from working with others, learning from them, and befriending them. Don't let those principles or values become barriers to interacting productively or respectfully with others. Hold your beliefs close. They make you uniquely capable of offering the world something only you can provide.

As our world grows more interconnected, there's a pressure to find common ground. Common ground is valuable and necessary. It can also be dangerous if it means trading in a strongly held personal belief or conviction for acceptance. Just because Western countries might be more comfortable with conflict, doesn't mean their leaders have a license to seek it out for no legitimate reason. Just because Eastern countries are less comfortable with conflict, doesn't mean their citizens should not defend their rights when trampled or their sovereignty is in jeopardy. The lens through which you or I might make that judgment will most assuredly be different, based on our cultural upbringing and experience.

Increasingly, our American culture is developing a pattern of behavior where we can no longer disagree agreeably and where differences are characterized with loaded terms. The irony is that in all the name calling and cancel-culture, we actually create more distance between ourselves. It's modern day segregation.

Consider what you can you do to be more flexible and more understanding without losing yourself and your ideals in the process. How can you better communicate your perspective in a way where others can appreciate it? What do you need to understand about their perspective and beliefs in order to work productively together?

▶ LESSON 20

We'll find the best ideas and achieve better outcomes if we stop thinking uniformity is the key. You don't have to give up your own personal moral convictions or religious beliefs to be culturally competent. Don't convert everyone around you to your way of thinking, but likewise, don't let them expect you to conform either. Be passionate about your beliefs but willing to challenge your assumptions.

Exercise grace and humility. Apologize.
Laugh at yourself. Find common ground.

ABOUT THE AUTHOR

JESSICA STONE is a 20 year veteran of local, national and international newsrooms where she has covered the intersection of politics and business around the world. Her work has appeared in the *South China Morning Post, Yahoo Finance, Stansberry Research, USA Today*, and the nation's FOX and CBS radio & television stations. Jessica's journalistic curiosity and passion to understand have taken her to five continents to work alongside a variety of cultures around the world. She spent seven years covering U.S.-China relations while serving as a White House Correspondent for *China Global Television Network*. During that time, she covered the rise of President Xi Jinping. She accompanied President Barack Obama to Brazil to cover how American foreign policy there diverged from China's. She was also the first CGTN correspondent to travel with President Donald Trump for a state visit to China in 2017. Jessica also produced the CGTN documentary, *Oil Sands at a Crossroads*,[1] about Chinese investment in Canadian energy. **She has interviewed former California Governor Arnold Schwarzenegger and former presidential candidates, including John Kerry, John Edwards, John McCain, Mitt Romney, Barack Obama, and Donald Trump.** She has reported from the military commissions at Guantanamo Bay, Cuba, the 2010 earthquake aftermath in Port-au-Prince, Haiti and spent two months covering the war in Afghanistan in 2009. These days, she lives with her family of four in Washington D.C. where she continues to apply her cultural competency skills to meaningful debates both on the world stage and across the dinner table.

---

1 https://www.youtube.com/watch?v=LsyEnkb0Gn0